CULINARY MAGIC OF THE EMIRATES

WHISPERED THROUGH TRADITIONAL STORIES

ALEXANDRA VON HAHN

Published by **MOTIVATE PUBLISHING**

DUBAI
Media One Tower, Dubai Media City
PO Box 2331, Dubai, UAE
Tel: (+971 4) 427 3000
Fax: (+971 4) 428 2268
books@motivate.ae
www.booksarabia.com

ABU DHABI
Makateb Building, 9th Street, Al Zahiyah
PO Box 43072, Abu Dhabi, UAE
Tel: (+971 2) 657 3493

LONDON
Acre House, 11/15 William Road,
London NW1 3ER

DIRECTORS: Obaid Humaid Al Tayer, Ian Fairservice
GENERAL MANAGER: Chris Capstick
EDITOR: Aswathy Sathish
PROJECT MANAGER: Malda Smadi
SENIOR DESIGNER: Noel de la Pena

British Library Cataloguing-in-Publication Data.
A catalogue record for this book is available from the British Library.

ISBN: 978 1 86063 467 3

NATIONAL MEDIA COUNCIL APPROVAL NUMBER: MC-02-01-0772213

CULINARY MAGIC OF THE

EMIRATES

WHISPERED THROUGH TRADITIONAL STORIES

ALEXANDRA VON HAHN

PREFACE

My first posting as a German Diplomat's wife was in Sana'a, the capital of Yemen in the Middle East. I came to realize quite quickly that my new role was to entertain guests whose palates had developed a yen for the best.

I was nowhere near being able to offer these sophisticated visitors the type of cuisine they had grown accustomed to. At the time, my idea of a fine dinner was empanadas, tomato cucumber onion salad, and mangoes and papayas for dessert. During my one-year stay in Yemen, I began a quest to refine my culinary capacities. Throughout my life as a diplomat's wife, this quest has continuously fuelled my desire to learn all I could about the food culture in the countries where I have lived.

Our last diplomatic posting was in the United Arab Emirates. In this country, I was made aware that food, simple yet tasty food, could be as satisfying if not more so, if shared with family and friends. The Emiratis have shown me that tradition is what makes a meal special. During my five-year stay in the Emirates I have witnessed this constantly. In fact, I became fascinated with Emirati food rituals and welcoming ceremonies. I thought it was quite fitting that as a parting gesture from the diplomatic circle, I should share what the Emiratis have so kindly and generously taught me.

With this in mind, I chose to share the recipes given to me by twenty-seven great cooks found throughout the vast and diverse expanse of the United Arab Emirates. In doing so, I have shared the spices, exotic local plants and herbs that these Emirati cooks use in their daily cooking. I have also divulged what motivated the Emirati Bedouins to have cooked the dishes they created forty to fifty years ago, which still result in delicious meals that are adapted to the modern Emirati's needs.

Why is Emirati cuisine becoming a symbol of national identity in the United Arab Emirates? Why is the international community so fascinated and intrigued by the art of traditional Emirati cooking when we have convenience foods readily available?

You will learn how easy it is for you to recreate the authentic recipes within your own home, garden, backyard or even in the desert. You will be inspired to recreate original traditional Emirati dishes which you, your family and friends will be ecstatic about. You will also discover the reasons behind Emirati Bedouin food rituals which include food harmony and blessing of the dishes. Luxuriate in the food preparation which always includes smelling, tasting, touching and observing when buying, preparing and cooking these authentic dishes steeped in the fascinating culture of the Emirati people.

Through the extraordinary openness of all the Emirati women and chefs whom I interviewed for this cookbook, one thing became clear: all had a special wish—to have their stories and recipes passed on to everyone passionate about cooking. Collectively they have left a legacy of Emirati values through their food rituals. Now you can experience the same culinary magic through this cookbook.

There is one exception: I decided to include one non-Emirati executive chef in this cookbook for a very simple reason. He is well-known for his delectable and innovative Emirati sweets. His name is Danny Kattar, and he works at the Intercontinental Hotel in Abu Dhabi (at the time of the interview). His passion is to design light desserts resulting in the most divine fusions between traditional Emirati sweets and Lebanese desserts.

ALEXANDRA VON HAHN

CONTENTS

Preface.... vi
Introduction to Emirati Food Rituals.... xii

MARIAM AL KAABI.... 8
Chicken Biryani
Machbous Rubyan
Dajaj Murraq
Thareed
Bzar
Rgaag
Legeimat

UMM MOHAMMED.... 20
Harees
Rgaag

NOORA ABDULRAHMAN ALMULLA ALZAROUNI.... 24
Bedouin Lamb Ghouzy

FATIMA ABDULLAH AHMED AL DHANHANI.... 32
Bedouin Machbous Laham

AZZA AL QUBAISI.... 36
Bedouin Sehnah with Rice
Bedouin Clams, Mussels and Spicy Tomato Sauce

NAJAT SAYED AL HASHEMI.... 46
Tahta Dajaj
Tahta Khodhar

SALHA AL SHAMSI.... 50
Margooga
Dhen Kheneen
Homemade Butter
Balaleet
Mohalla
Khanfaroush

FATIMA AL GHUFLI.... 56
Bedouin Sherry Fish and Rice
Semach Magli with Rice
Bedouin Coffee
Chai Karak
Balaleet

FATIMA AL QUBAISI.... 62
Machicha Fish with Rice

NADIA AL HAMELI.... 68
Mohalla

MARIAM AND SALIMA AL YAMMAHI.... 74
Young Lamb in an Oven Pit
Al Yammahi Rice Dish
Al Yammahi Bzar
Harees

KHAWLA AL ZAABI.... 82
Bedouin Wild Ghaf Salad
Whole Roasted Fish
Saloona with Maleh

MARIAM HAMMAT.... 90
Aseeda with Carrots

MONA AL ZAABI.... 94
Chbaab
Bedouin Khameer

HANAN RASHID HAMDAN AL SHOOKRI 98

Helba

Haba Al Hamra

SHAIKHA MOHAMED AL KAABI'S 'MEYLAS' FOOD TRUCK 102

Batheetha

Legeimat

MARIAM ABDULLAH AL FALASI 108

Mamshoora Maleh

Maleh

Tahta Maleh

HALIMA AL ATTAR 116

Jasheed

Bedouin Camel Milk and Date Smoothie

CHEF KHULOOD ATIQ 120

Balaleet Dish

Shorbat Adas

Harees Soup

CHEF MUSABBEH AL KAABI 124

Muhallabia

Halib Jamal

Bzar

Bedouin Camel Ghouzy

CHEF LATIFA MASOOD 132

Achaar Tamat

Achaar Liamun

Achaar Hamba

EXECUTIVE CHEF DANNY KATTAR 136

Aish Al Saraya

Ithmaliyeh Noodles

AISHA AL MEHREZI 142

Emirati Coffee

NASRA ALBALOOSHI 146

Haba Hamra

Sago Pudding

ZAHRA AL NAHDI 152

Qahwa

Legeimat

AYSHA KHAMIES AL KHADDEIM 156

Khabees

Rangila

LATIFA TAYEEB AL KHAJA 160

Khabees

Acknowledgements 164

INTRODUCTION TO EMIRATI FOOD RITUALS

TRADITIONAL EMIRATI FOOD IS THE IDENTITY AND THE HEART OF THE UNITED ARAB EMIRATES.

Anyone who has visited or plans to visit the United Arab Emirates will discover the fascinating undercurrent of Emirati hospitality and their food culture. It is expressed in their daily lives and at all official, private and religious events. We should realize that they are indeed of immense value and importance to everyone who is interested in the Emirati food rituals. Although the food rituals mentioned herein represent only a glimpse of the whole, they still are of great importance for the next generation of Emiratis and everyone else who is interested in learning and appreciating what Emirati families have left as a legacy to all of us.

You will often see variations in the spelling of main dishes, breads, spices, pickles, beverages, soups and desserts in cookbooks, online cookery sites and recipes found amongst the Emirati families. For instance, the popular chicken stew known as *machbous diyay* is often seen spelled as *machboos*, *machbus*, *machkbous*, etc. It's easy to see why it can be confusing. The more you cook, the more you will become used to the different variations of the spellings for the same dish.

EMIRATI CUISINE

In the past, food was very limited due to the extremely arid and harsh desert conditions and lack of produce. The Bedouins who lived along the coast survived on a diet based on camel milk, dates and fresh fish. While the Bedouins who lived inland consumed dried fish, dates, fruits, vegetables and locally grown cereals. They raised chicken, fowl, camels, sheep and goats. The consumption of camel meat was reserved for very special occasions as the camel provided milk from which butter and laban (buttermilk) were produced, and also because the camel was their only means of transportation.

Leafy greens were taken from indigenous trees such as the wild ghaf tree which today is the national tree of the United Arab Emirates. Ghaf leaves were either chopped and sprinkled with lime juice and eaten raw or they were cooked and the semi-bitter flavours developed during the cooking process. From the arta tree, also known as the machicha tree, the young arta's bitter-sour shoots were chopped up and pounded using a mortar and pestle to ensure softer chewing. Radish tails and a variety of aquatic green plants were consumed as well. In fact, the ladies I interviewed for this cookbook still serve leaves from the ghaf and young shoots from the arta trees.

Before the discovery of oil, and before the seven sheikhdoms joined together to form the United Arab Emirates, they depended on pearl trade as their main source of income. The traders travelled in dhows to the neighbouring countries and as far as India; they brought back spices, rice, clothes, kitchen utensils, pots and pans, and much more. During this period, the Emirati cuisine was strongly influenced by Middle Eastern and Asian countries.

Bedouins are very talented and inventive with the resources available to them and have developed many dishes that Emiratis still enjoy today such as *harees* (porridge with meat), *ghouzy* (grilled or steamed lamb, goat or camel), *maleh* (salted fish), *margooga* (stew mixed with soft bread dough), *farni* (rice pudding) and breads such as the *chbaab*, *rgaag* and *khameer*.

To leaven the bread, Emiratis made their own version of yeast. They fermented dates under the sun and used it as a rising agent for some of their breads. *Thareed*, a meat stew layered with *rgaag* (paper thin bread) and sweet dates are a natural symbol of hospitality. *Batheetha* (dates and roasted flour) is a popular comfort dessert and is also offered as a sign of hospitality.

BZAR (EMIRATI SPICE)

One must not forget the popular Emirati *bzar* which is a spice mixture often composed of chilli, coriander, cassia, cumin, black pepper, star anise, garlic, fenugreek, ginger, turmeric, dried lime, nutmeg, fennel and sometimes dried mountain mushrooms from Fujairah. Cardamom was traditionally considered to only belong in sweet dishes and was only added much later into the *bzar* spice mixture. Saffron is added to dishes, however, and not blended into the *bzar* spice mixture. Women considered it important to harmonize the dishes by balancing the taste with their own spice mixture.

A well balanced, harmonious *bzar* spice mixture is another important sign of hospitality. Traditionally, spices were bought whole, washed and left to dry in the sun until they exuded a strong fragrance. They were then pounded and stored in jars in order to protect the essential oils from escaping. Today, many Emirati families still buy whole spices which they roast and then either pound or use an electric spice grinder to powder. Their unique homemade *bzar* mixture is used for meat, poultry, bread and rice dishes. Emiratis are often seen selling *bzar* at traditional festivals and markets.

If you happen to attend any Emirati traditional festival, you will be able to buy unique compositions of *bzar* from the Emirati women who still enjoy preparing homemade *bzar* mixtures. I recommend that you also try to find *bzar* with roasted mountain mushrooms, a delicacy from the mountains of Fujairah.

EMIRATI FAMILY VALUES

Emirati families started long ago to teach their children about their values. They learn by observing the family's behavioral patterns, through their daily life actions and participation. Every special occasion, such as Ramadan, weddings, birthdays, deaths and other family festivities are all based on strong family values that create an invisible common communication network amongst Emiratis.

Family values are transmitted through very clear messages and intentions. Values are applied every day and are always part of their daily routine, during meal time and daily prayers. Their words, dress code and actions are consistent, and these themselves are a very noble art of communication. Family values are passed from one generation to another throughout the United Arab Emirates and those living, working and studying abroad exercise and respect the continuity of these family values as well. In fact, each member is held accountable for their family's values to ensure that through this commitment and responsibility they are able to depend on each other as one large family.

It takes many years to create a legacy for the next generation. In fact, it is a lifelong commitment. This is accomplished through storytelling, especially when sitting together on the floor in a circle around a plaited palm leaf matt called *sarrut* or modern tablecloths laden with traditional dishes which are always shared. Sharing is also part of the family values system.

Today, empowered Emirati women have an active role in leadership at work and within the family. For example, women have repositioned themselves as active educators of their children in addition to their career so that their family values become an integral part of their children's stability in society. Women have noticed that through the multiculturalism in the United Arab Emirates, their children need far more attention and acknowledgment in order to preserve the Emirati values.

I was impressed by Fatima Al Ghufli, one of the participants in this book, who explained the following about her family values: 'The patriarchal order in my family plays a strong traditional role but is modified through conscious adjustments and adaptations to the modern way of life. Educated women enter the workforce and earn their own income which remains their personal source of earning.'

Get-togethers with other women are an important feature of traditional family values that also help in maintaining a network amongst the women. This was best described by Latifa Tayeeb Al Khaja, another participant, during her interview with me: 'Henna get-togethers are a woman's time to reconnect by creating a deeper bond with herself and empower others. We take time for ourselves to feel emotionally nourished by other women while having our hands dyed with henna.'

EMIRATI FOOD RITUALS

Emirati food rituals are not only adaptable to modern lifestyle but most importantly they are the signature of Emirati culture. They make a big difference in how each person experiences and expresses appreciation and gratitude for the meal. Traditional Emirati rituals are commonly associated with celebration, and are deeply symbolic. They nourish and satisfy the soul, strengthen family ties, give meaning to mealtime sharing, focus the attention to the present moment and a heightened level of awareness and finally bring families closer to Allah.

RAMADAN

Ramadan is declared when the crescent of the moon is sighted, and the ninth month of the Islamic lunar calendar has begun. It lasts from twenty-nine to thirty days. During this period of fasting and prayer, Muslims refrain from eating and drinking from dawn till sunset. Fasting during Ramadan is one of the Five Pillars of Islam, and is mandatory for everyone who has reached the puberty and is healthy. Exemptions from fasting are made for pregnant women, the elderly and the chronically ill.

Ramadan is a time of reflection and charity. Many people sponsor charity tents that include traditional Emirati dishes to those in need. In the Emirates many mosques serve iftar *saem*. The food is donated to the mosques by Emiratis as well as the international community. Food is served to all those present and those who wish to eat a meal at the mosque. About thirty minutes before the call of the muezzin declaring iftar, it is impossible to hail a taxi and public transportation comes to a halt. Drivers make sure to reach a nearby mosque to be able to arrive on time and enjoy iftar with the community.

The Ramadan food fasting ritual is based upon two meals: one taken early in the morning before dawn known as *suhoor* and the other after sunset known as iftar. Predawn meals provide enough energy for the long fasting hours which last until shortly after sunset. A traditional *suhoor* menu is composed of foods such as fruit juices, milk, water, dates, lentil soup, bread, fruit, vegetables and *harees*, the Emirati food of choice. It is a warm porridge composed of slow cooked wheat with or without meat.

Breaking the fast shortly after sunset is traditionally done with three dates and water before moving to the other dishes during iftar such as *harees*, lentil soup, bread, rice with meat or fish, vegetables, fruits, sweet desserts, Emirati beverages, Emirati coffee and *karak* tea. You can enjoy any or all of these dishes from amongst the recipes found in this book. To celebrate the end of Ramadan, an event of several days takes place called Eid al-Fitr and as with all occasions, it is celebrated with family, friends and neighbours. The traditional ritual calls for sitting on the floor in a circle so as to connect with one another, and share and savour exquisite traditional dishes.

If you happen to be in the United Arab Emirates just about one month prior to Ramadan, you will be swept away by the aromatic fragrances of nuts, spices, sweet Arabic pastries, while Emirati families are stocking up in anticipation of hosting and entertaining during this very special occasion. Food and ingredients such as rice, wheat, grains, sugar, dates, date syrup, paste and juice, nuts, rose water, orange blossom water and spices are all bought in bulk quantities. Pre-orders of a great selection and large quantities of Arabic sweet pastries and cakes must be taken care of as well.

A lifetime experience, and one not to be missed especially during Ramadan shopping hours, is when you go to the Spice Souk in Deira, Dubai. The exotic fragrances will slowly impress and entice you to savour the traditional spices, rose petals, traditional Indian and local medicinal plant based products, incense, oud (aromatic resin) and baskets and bags filled to the rim with herbs.

The preselection of poultry, lamb, beef and camel takes place at their favourite farmer. The livestock are left with the farmer to be fed with quality feed until they are ready to be consumed during iftar. As Mona Al Zaabi explained during her interview for this book, 'During Ramadan fresh dishes are prepared daily, and iftar is the time when there is a lot of hosting and home entertainment for their large families, friends, guests and neighbours. It is also a time for the women and men who enjoy cooking to showcase their cooking talents, which is another gesture of the Emirati hospitality.

EMIRATI COFFEE OR *QAHWA*

Bedouins have successfully passed on the art of celebrating, honouring and welcoming their guests with coffee. Known as Emirati coffee or *qahwa*, it reflects the rituals and signs of traditional Emirati hospitality.

Bedouins have long treasured their coffee rituals. It is part of their essential and elegant way of greeting, welcoming and honouring their families and friends, and the coffee acts as a catalyst in establishing connections. Emiratis still continue to respect this tradition to this day. Their gatherings are always supported and beautified with coffee poured from a *dallah* (the traditional brass coffee pot with a long spout) with the left hand and served with the right hand. The receiver holds the demi cup (also known as a demitasse cup, or *finjan*, a small, handleless coffee cup) in the right hand, and slowly sips from it. The coffee is poured to only one-third of the cup, so as to honour the person by them never having to experience a mouth burn. The host or hostess always makes sure that everyone is served again unless the demi cup is jiggled from right to left—a sign that no more coffee is desired.

When you return the demi cup, Mariam Al Kaabi, another participant, said to me, 'You must say: May God greet you—*Hayyach Allah*.'

Coffee drinking is an elegant way to foster get-togethers resulting in renewed friendships, reconnection and getting to know each other; an essential part of establishing friendships and all this through the magic of coffee rituals. *Qahwa* is the magic hospitality beverage that has digestive virtues and so is appreciated after meals. It is the sign of hospitality, a sign of welcoming a guest, and is served with dates for every occasion, upon arrival and departure of guests.

Bedouins learned to benefit from their date palm tree that not only provided them with dates, fronds, wood and trunks used for the construction of their homes, but they also created their own coffee from date pits. Bedouins collected date pits, let them dry under the sun and delicately roasted them until they exuded an elegant mild roasted woody fragrance, which they mixed with pounded cardamom and cooked on a very low fire. Some families added pounded ginger shortly before serving their coffee based on roasted date pits.

Later the roasting of date pits gave way to the Indian coffee beans, which are still used today, often mixed with a great selection of high quality green coffee beans imported to the United Arab Emirates.

EMIRATI FOOD QUALITY INSPECTION RITUALS

Bedouins mastered the art of quality food inspection through some unique and very effective methods—touching, smelling, tasting and looking—before they consider buying meat, seafood, fruits, vegetables, dates, nuts, spices, coffee, tea, rice, cereals, tobacco and more.

My friend Fatima Al Qubaisi, another participant, showed me how to apply the Bedouin food inspection method which is in fact still exercised today in the same way as the Bedouins used to do it in the past. She said, 'Emirati women know their food rituals.' The dry fish chosen by Fatima was touched, smelled, tasted (by quickly and discreetly placing the finger that touched the fish onto her tongue) and last but not least, the dry stockfish was finally inspected visually from all sides before she bought it.

EMIRATI MEALS

For breakfast, Emiratis usually have breads such as *chbaab*, *rgaag* or *khameer* served with date syrup, dates, white cream cheese, *laban* or tea and honey from the mountains of Fujairah or Oman.

Lunch is the most important meal for Emiratis. A variety of dishes are served such as *machbous*, *maleh*, *jasheed*, *margooga*, *tahta maleh*, *thareed* and *ghouzy* just to name a few. Dinner usually also consisted of the same or similar dishes. Mealtimes are when they socialize and reconnect with one another.

Desserts or *fualah* often consist of *legeimat*, a one-biter doughnut drizzled with date syrup or honey and sprinkled with sesame seeds, *khanfaroush*, a three-biter thick fried pancake drizzled with date syrup, *khabeesa*, toasted flour crumbs mixed with sugar, saffron and cardamom, and *batheetha*, semolina with pureed dates mixed with cardamom and Emirati clarified butter or ghee.

At the end of any meal, it is customary to be served Emirati coffee or tea and dates.

BLESSING THE FOOD AND OTHER EATING RITUALS

Before sitting down for a meal, hands are washed and prayers are conducted either before or after the meal depending on the time of the day.

Mariam Al Kaabi and Zahra Al Nahdi, who were both interviewed for this book, conveyed the importance of blessing the food when their families, friends and guests are seated on the floor on a round plaited mat. Blessing of the food is said by everyone in unison, 'Bismillah' or 'In the name of God', expressing appreciation and gratitude for the meal.

Mariam told me that blessing the food causes the dishes to taste better. 'Food,' she said, 'is one of Allah's greatest gifts to us.' After the blessing of the food, the host or hostess says '*Samhuna ad*' or 'Forgive us'. This is to let the guests know the modesty of the food display despite the mat or table being laden with dishes. The guests respond with '*Masmulla*' or 'You are forgiven'.

Zahra explained, 'If you are invited by Emiratis, the host or hostess will serve you the food on your plate. The more food on your plate is a sign that you are a guest of honour. You will most likely be told that you have not eaten, despite having eaten and you are no longer hungry. This is when you wash your hands elegantly in a bowl, if provided, which is a clear sign that you no longer wish to eat. If the washing bowl is not available you may say '*Akramch*' or 'May Allah honour you'.

Food is eaten with the right hand. The left hand is reserved for bodily hygiene. Each person assigns themselves a section of the rice platter, often placed in the center of the *sarrut* or plaited mat surrounded by smaller side dishes. The assigned section of the rice platter and of the other plates is a sign of harmony and order. It is a sign of courtesy to ask for permission to pick a piece of meat that is further away from you or if the piece of meat is only on your side. This food ritual encourages sharing, respect and teamwork according to Mariam.

You are going to be impressed by the mastery of how Emiratis are able to scoop up a 'mouthful' or *logma*, a food ritual explained to me by Halima Al Attar, another participant. Scooping a little rice, meat, sauce and vegetable into the hand is followed by pressing the collected food several times against the palm of the hand using all four fingers until the food is shaped into a small ball referred to as a 'mouthful'. You are now ready to bring the hand close to your mouth and use your thumb to elegantly push the food into your mouth without causing the food to drop or dirty your mouth.

From another interviewee, Salha Al Shamsi, I learned three seating positions which is a ritual introduced by Prophet Mohammed (peace be upon Him) in order to feel the earth given to us by Allah. Everyone is equal when sitting on the floor. Any of the following three sitting positions may be used when sitting on the floor, while ensuring that the soles of the feet do not show—legs crossed over each other and knees flat on the floor; one leg bent flat on the floor, foot is towards the body, the other leg held vertically outwards with the knee bent at ninety degrees; and legs and feet tucked under the body to one side.

Salha also revealed that Prophet Mohammed (peace be upon Him) passed on the legacy that in the second sitting position, there is less consumption of food due to the leg being held vertically outwards with the knee at ninety degrees, thereby permitting some abdominal space left for water and air. This position is therefore useful for natural weight and health maintenance.

MARIAM AL KAABI AND HER FAMILY

AL FOAH, AL AIN

I met Mariam Al Kaabi and her wonderful family after being introduced to them by her niece whom I'd met at a piano concert a few weeks earlier. My family and I drove to their villa in Al Ain with the thought of getting to know them first before being permitted to learn about their delicious traditional recipes. We were welcomed straight away by her large, warm-hearted family.

I was taken aback and touched by their hospitality, politeness, and generosity, especially since we were invited in for the most important meal of the day—lunch!

We were kindly told to remove our shoes at the entrance of the house and invited to be seated to share their food which was placed on a tablecloth on the floor. It was a delicious array of grapes, apples, oranges, sliced watermelon, mangoes and rich, aromatic home-made Arabic coffee served from a *zamzamiyah* which is a traditional coffee pot. There were biscuits, dates, traditional dishes and sweets. It's true that the eyes are important when eating because the colours were utterly amazing and the delightful aromas and fragrances quite simply blew me away.

Mariam, dressed in her traditional Bedouin abaya (black cloak draped over her head and dress) and her fingertips dipped in henna, served us a wonderfully rich blend of Arabic coffee.

I observed with curious fascination the striking presentation of her traditional apparel, which included a golden *burqa* providing a partial facial covering to protect against exposure to the sun and weather elements.

I had a fascinating conversation with Mariam who went on to explain that older women in the United Arab Emirates continue to embrace the importance of covering important facial areas whereas women of the current generation decline to wear the *burqa*. Mariam embellished that women express their own preference for the style of *burqa* they wear and also for the importance of distinguishing marital status.

A golden Indian material which darkens with age and contact with the wearer's skin, the *burqa* has openings of varied sizes for suitable visibility by the bearer. These openings abridge the nose with a cylindrical piece of wood called an *al seif.* With considerable enthusiasm Mariam demonstrated how she puts on the *burqa* by tying twisted strings on either side back behind her head. She observed that for special occasions such as weddings, the strings are golden and silver in colour.

Mariam emphasized that women now wear the *burqa* primarily for aesthetic reasons appreciated and respected by those wearing the *burqa* and the observer. With conviction Mariam exclaimed that *burqas* with a larger opening are intended for younger women while those with smaller openings were meant for the elderly women!

Mariam went on to serve the coffee with her left hand while holding the miniature cups in her right, and filled them up to a third in order to let her guests drink the coffee without burning their tongues. It was a delicious, mild-strength coffee fragranced with cardamom and served without sugar—I had my coffee cup filled three times!

Mariam taught me to say '*Tawal Allah Umrich*' which means 'May God give you long life', and another very important word '*Mashkurah*' which means 'Thank you' when returning the coffee cup back to the hostess. This is something I will now always say after my Emirati coffee.

Don't forget Emirati coffee does not taste like regular coffee; in fact it is slightly bitter, spicy and aromatic. With the addition of cardamom and saffron, the coffee takes on a yellow hue. The taste of Emirati coffee grew on me!

Chicken Biryani

SERVES 4–6

INGREDIENTS FOR CHICKEN MIXTURE:

2 kg chicken, cut into pieces
4½ cups oil
1 large onion, peeled and diced
1 tsp saffron powder
2 tbsp cardamom pods, shelled and ground
2 tbsp *bzar* (see page 15)
4 tbsp grated ginger
4 tsp tomato paste
1 tbsp cumin powder
½ tbsp chilli powder
2 dried chilli peppers
4 tbsp water
4½ tsp salt
1 tbsp turmeric powder
1 tsp ground black pepper
½ tsp ground cinnamon

INGREDIENTS FOR RICE:

6 cups rice
1 tbsp salt
2 tbsp vegetable oil
½ cup pine nuts
½ cup cashew nuts
½ cup pistachios
½ cup *zereshk* (red-coloured dried Iranian barberries)

Rinse rice well and drain in a colander. Place rice in bowl and cover with water. Leave for 2 hours. Drain and place rice back into bowl and cover with water until ready to cook (rinsing, soaking and re-soaking rice removes a lot of starch and makes the cooked rice light and fluffy).

Marinate chicken in 4 teaspoons of salt and 3 teaspoons of turmeric powder for 30 minutes. In a large skillet, heat 2 cups of vegetable oil and fry the chicken pieces until light brown in colour. Remove from oil and set aside.

Add the remaining ½ cup of oil to another skillet and fry the diced onion, chilli powder, cumin, and cardamom until light brown in colour. Add the grated ginger, tomato paste, garlic, *bzar*, saffron powder, dried chilli, cumin powder and mix well. Stir and gently fry for 2 minutes. Add 4 tbsp of water (one tbsp at a time). Reduce heat and simmer until thick and smooth.

Add the chicken pieces and ½ teaspoon of salt, 1 teaspoon of ground black pepper and ½ teaspoon of ground cinnamon. Cover and simmer over very low heat until chicken is tender, approximately 35–45 minutes. Stir regularly to prevent sauce from sticking to the skillet. If sauce begins to stick add a little water.

In the meantime, boil 3 litres of water, add 2 tablespoons of vegetable oil and 1 tablespoon of salt. Add the 6 cups of drained rice and cook over medium heat until half cooked. Remove from heat, drain and place on top of the chicken mixture. Cover and cook over low heat for 20 minutes or until rice is fluffy and ready to eat.

Gently mix the rice with the chicken mixture. In a pan add pine nuts, cashew nuts, pistachios and *zereshk*, and roast over very low heat until light golden-brown in colour. The *zereshk* will become dark red. Extra care must be taken not to burn the *zereshk*. Garnish the chicken biryani with the roasted nut mixture, and serve hot.

The Emirates and the Gulf area are well known for their delicious and personalized versions of Machbous.

Machbous Rubyan

RICE WITH SHRIMPS

SERVES 4–6

INGREDIENTS FOR RICE:

3 cups Basmati rice
water

INGREDIENTS FOR SHRIMPS:

1 kg shrimps, rinsed, shelled and deveined
1 tbsp onion, peeled and chopped
1 tsp chilli powder
1 tsp cumin powder
½ tsp garlic, peeled and crushed
½ tsp ginger, peeled and crushed
1 tomato, chopped

INGREDIENTS FOR SAUCE:

1 tsp turmeric powder
½ cup vegetable oil
1 tsp garlic, peeled and crushed
1 tsp ginger, peeled and crushed
1 tomato, chopped
½ tsp ground black pepper
2 tsp *bzar* (see page 15)
2 *loumi* (dried lime)
2 tsp salt
2½ cups water

Rinse and drain the rice. Place rice in a bowl, cover with water and leave for 2 hours. Drain in a colander and place the rice back into bowl and cover with water until you are ready to cook (rinsing and soaking rice removes excess starch and makes cooked rice light and fluffy). You will need to keep 3 cups of rice water for later.

Place the shrimps in large pot. Add the onion, chilli powder, cumin, garlic, ginger and tomato. Cook over low heat until the shrimps change colour and become light pink. Transfer shrimp mixture to a large pot, separating the shrimps to stop the cooking.

In large saucepan heat the vegetable oil. Add turmeric, garlic, ginger, tomato, black pepper, *bzar*, *loumi*, salt and ½ cup of water. Bring to a boil. Add cooked shrimps and pour in remaining 2 cups of water. Bring to a boil, cover the saucepan and simmer for 5 minutes. While sauce is simmering, stir in the drained rice and bring to a boil. Add the 3 cups of reserved rice water, cover and simmer for 20 minutes. The rice is done when it is tender and you cannot feel a hard centre. Remove from heat and keep covered for 5 minutes. Garnish with fresh chopped coriander and fresh lemon or lime wedges and serve warm.

Chicken Stew with potatoes and vegetables is a very popular dish in the UAE and my recipe goes back to when we were living the lifestyle of Emirati Bedouins.

Dajaj Murraq

CHICKEN STEW

SERVES 4–6

1 kg whole chicken cut into 8–10 pieces
½ tsp turmeric powder
⅓ cup vegetable oil
2 onions, peeled and diced
2 tsp cardamom, crushed
1 tsp cumin powder
½ tsp chilli powder
1 kg zucchini, cut into slices
1 large potato, peeled and cut into cubes
1 large carrot, peeled and cut into slices
1 *loumi* (dried lime), crushed
6 cups water
2 tsp salt
1 tsp cinnamon powder
1 tsp crushed garlic cloves
1 tsp crushed ginger
4 tbsp tomato paste
½ cup water
½ tsp saffron powder
1 cup chopped coriander (optional)

Sprinkle chicken with turmeric. Refrigerate for 30 minutes. In large deep pan, fry onions in oil until translucent. Add chilli powder, crushed cardamom and cumin and cook until spices become fragrant. Add chicken and cook over moderate heat until it begins to brown. Add cinnamon, garlic, ginger, tomato paste, ½ cup of water, saffron and mix well over moderate heat. Cover pan and cook until spices become fragrant. Add the vegetables, 6 cups of water and salt. Stir well and bring to a boil. Cover and simmer until the water is reduced by half and the chicken and vegetables are cooked. Remove from heat and leave covered for 5 minutes. Garnish with fresh chopped coriander (optional).

A hearty spiced chicken stew which is best served over rice. What's more, it's easy to prepare. My suggestion is to make more than what is called for; your friends and guests will appreciate it.

This recipe is a combination of paper-thin sheets of bread called rgaag which is layered with dajaj murraq or chicken stew (chicken can be replaced by lamb, beef or camel meat).

Thareed

PAPER-THIN SHEETS OF BREAD, RGAAG, LAYERED WITH DAJAJ MURRAQ

4 pieces *rgaag* (see page 16)
1 pot *dajaj murraq* (see page 14)
1 cup chopped coriander

Take the sheets of *rgaag* and break them into pieces. Add one layer of the bread (approximately one sheet of *rgaag* should be used for each layer) into a large, deep-sided dish and spoon some of the liquid from the stew over it. The bread should be soaked in the liquid. Add another layer of bread followed by more liquid. Repeat this step until all the bread has been used. Now spoon the rest of the chicken stew over it all. Garnish with coriander. Serve hot.

The different textures of this traditional Emirati dish make *thareed* irresistible. Soaked layers of thin bread and meaty stew make your mouth water.

Bzar

EMIRATI SPICE MIX

1 cup cumin seeds
1 cup black peppercorns
1 cup coriander seeds
¼ cup chilli peppers, dried
½ cup dried yellow onion flakes
1 cup cinnamon sticks, broken into pieces
1 cup ginger (dry ginger pounded into small pieces, easier to grind later)
½ cup garlic cloves, peeled
¼ cup saffron threads
5 nutmeg seeds, broken into pieces
½ cup paprika powder
1 cup turmeric powder

Lightly dry-roast all spices (except turmeric and paprika) over low heat, stirring constantly with a wooden spoon until the spices give off a delicious fragrance and turn golden brown in colour. Remove from heat. Add turmeric and paprika powder and mix well. Allow spices to cool. Grind spices in a mortar and pestle or use an electric grinder. Store the ground spices in an airtight container, away from light. This *bzar* spice can be stored for up to one year.

Rgaag

PAPER-THIN BREAD

SERVES 6 -10

Rgaag is traditional, unleavened, paper-thin bread that the Emirates eat for breakfast, lunch and dinner. It's very popular during Ramadan. *Rgaag* (also spelled *rugag* or *rqaq*) is part of the *thareed* bread recipes and can be eaten hot and drizzled with oil and honey, date honey, eggs, herbs, ghee (clarified butter), cheese, zaatar, tomatoes, olives and spices.

The bread is made on a thin circular plate called a *tabi* and requires great skill to make it. The liquid dough is placed on the *tabi* over direct heat. The edges are carefully scraped using a spatula (a carpenter's spatula works well) then it's folded and served hot. It takes time and practice to master the art of making *rgaag*.

Mariam Al Kaabi prefers to use whole wheat flour. She insists that her *rgaag* tastes much more authentic using whole wheat flour.

2 kg whole wheat flour or brown flour
1 tsp salt
2–3 cups water, room temperature
1 bowl water for your hands
Tabi: large, thin, circular iron plate

Mix flour and salt in a bowl. Slowly add water to obtain a semi-liquid dough. It should be a thickness that allows it to easily spread on the *tabi*. Cover with a kitchen towel and leave to rest in a warm area for 30 minutes. Place *tabi* on a direct flame. When *tabi* is hot, dip your whole hand in water and take a handful of dough. Place it on the outer edge of the *tabi*. Spread the dough in a circular motion until you get to the centre of the *tabi*. Holes can be filled by dabbing a bit of dough over them. Using a carpenter's metal spatula, lift the bread once the edges are light brown and crisp. A steady hand will ensure that the *rgaag* doesn't break.

Traditionally, Emirati families exercised a gifting food ritual before the sunset prayers that I still enjoy today. The exchange of legeimat amongst our neighbours and friends.

Legeimat

ONE-BITE SOFT AND CRUNCHY DOUGHNUT

SERVES 8–12

This recipe is similar to our mini-doughnuts. They are delicate, crunchy and have been personalized by Mariam Al Kaabi. They differ from traditional *legeimat* recipes in that they contain no eggs. Adding powdered milk makes the *legeimat* smoother and lighter according to Mariam.

2 cups white flour
2 tbsp powdered milk
1 sachet (1 tbsp) instant yeast
1 tsp salt
1 tsp sugar
water as needed for a smooth and fluid dough
3 cups oil for frying
natural honey

Using your hands, mix all dry ingredients in a large bowl until there are no lumps. Add water until the dough is smooth and has become slightly liquid in consistency. Allow dough to rest, covered, for about 30 minutes. Heat oil in a deep pan over medium heat. Using your thumb, index and middle fingers lift the dough to create small balls and drop them into the oil. Turn the *legeimat* using a large metal spoon to get an even golden colour. Do not become discouraged if they are not perfectly round. You will get perfectly round *legeimat* the more you practice making them. Dip your fingers in water between each *legeimat*. Once the *legeimat* are gold in colour, drain on a paper towel. Transfer to a serving dish. Lace them with natural honey and eat while they are still hot.

Emiratis cannot live without their *legeimat*, which is one of their most popular desserts. *Legeimat* is especially well-received during the holy month of Ramadan and for weddings, birthdays and other special occasions.

UMM MOHAMMED
ABU DHABI

THE KORAN READER

I first met Umm Mohammed while interviewing my former neighbour Zahra Al Nahdi for my Emirati cookbook. Umm Mohammed in Arabic means 'mother of Mohammed'. At an early age, Umm Mohammed began teaching women of all ages to memorize the Koran. She thus became known as 'Umm Mohammed'. Today you can easily find Umm reading the Koran at the Qur'an Memorization Centre in Al Bateen for she is a very convincing reader with qualities worthy of Shakespearean actors!

Umm Mohammed is a petite woman from Bedouin background and originates from Abu Dhabi. Despite her small stature she has a strong and powerful personality. She can communicate directly and shows a lot of enthusiasm, self-respect and an equal measure of respect for others. I was impressed by Umm when I first saw her standing in front of her mansion waiting for me to pick her up. The interview took place at the home of our mutual friend Zahra Al Nahdi.

Umm sat in the front seat of my Land Cruiser and said: 'Alexandra, *yallah*' (in Arabic meaning 'fast' or 'let's go.') I smiled at her request and told her to buckle herself in first. She smiled and said: 'I am in Germany.' My friend had informed her that my husband worked at the German Embassy. We had not driven for five minutes when she said: 'Stop'. I stopped in front of the Al Bateen Mall where she jumped out of the car, raced into the mall and returned with a large bag of wheat kernels, gave me a big smile and said: 'Yallah!' Off we went to Zahra's villa where I prepared for both interviews.

I was glad that Zahra translated for me because Umm Mohammed was ready to demonstrate her ability to cook while dictating her recipes, multitasking at a very fast pace! The art of cooking Emirati dishes, as stated by Umm Mohammed, is to cook like her mother and according to her it is very important to be conscious of high quality and fresh ingredients for the dishes. Every day she would go to the market and supermarket to select the freshest fruits, vegetables, meat and dry ingredients for her family's daily lunch, which is still considered to be the most important meal of the day.

'Women occupied a very important position in Bedouin society, and that is still evident today in our modern United Arab Emirates,' explained Umm Mohammed. She went on to say: 'Women still raise their children themselves. However, many Emirati women in modern United Arab Emirates have traditional dishes prepared by their Indian cooks who learned the recipes from Emirati women who hired them, women who still prefer to have Emirati traditional food prepared, cooked and served to their families.' Umm Mohammed continued: 'When Emirati families gather to eat their daily meals in a circle on the carpeted floors, they feel that eating in a circle brings connectivity amongst the family members. This is a treasured legacy from the time when we lived our lives as Bedouins.'

Umm decided to sit on a small stool in front of a large pot. The pot was placed on a mobile floor gas stove. It contained hot water and lamb in preparation for the *harees* dish. This dish is composed of thoroughly cooked wheat kernels and lamb meat including the head. The long cooking gives *harees* a porridge-like consistency.

Umm Mohammed continued to say: 'We still follow most of our traditional social customs and we look forward to gatherings around the fire, or at our majlis (sitting area with decorated cushions) sharing our experiences or stories while cherishing the tasty dishes. This would be followed by slowly sipping our Emirati coffee and tea. To end the gatherings, the host, hostess or a designated member of the family passes burning incense to each guest and to the members of the family to be fanned by hand towards one's chest while facing each other. This would in turn be followed by sharing a wide spectrum of fragrant perfumes and perfumed oils.

At this point Umm Mohammed was vigorously stirring her *harees* while listening to her friend Zahra explaining how to make *legeimat*. I noticed Umm's facial expression becoming very concerned and her attentive gaze was no longer focused on stirring the *harees*. Instead, she maintained that Zahra was baking *khanfaroush* and not *legeimat*. Both women had a long discussion regarding the name and shape of the dough when dropped into the hot oil.

According to Zahra, when the dough is cut into round and flat circles it is called *legeimat*. According to Umm Mohammed, when the dough is squeezed from between the fingers into the hot oil it is called *legeimat* and Zahra's flat disked pieces are called *khanfaroush*.

I decided to taste Zahra's *legeimat* which was drizzled with a generous amount of date syrup and sprinkled with sesame seeds. These exquisite flat-disked one-biters melted in my mouth and left a light taste of cardamom and saffron. They are delicious and you will probably come back to finish the bowl!

Zahra informed me that it is common to have long discussions about whether this delightful item is *legeimat* or *khanfaroush*. I have noticed that in the United Arab Emirates the round shaped one-biter dough is referred to as *legeimat* and is drizzled with date syrup and sprinkled with sesame seeds. No matter what the name, they're scrumptious!

Harees

WHEAT PORRIDGE WITH LAMB

SERVES 6 -8

Harees is one of the most popular and savoured dishes in the United Arab Emirates for weddings, Eid, Ramadan and all other special occasions. It is filling and considered to be comfort food. *Harees* is composed of wheat and meat and is stirred until the meat is dissolved into the wheat. It has the consistency of porridge.

Umm Mohammed told me that her parents used to cook *harees* as a team. Her mother would prepare and cook the *harees* until the stirring step. It was at this stage that her father and all the other men in her family would take turns stirring the *harees* until smooth, thick and ready to be topped with *dhen kheneen* or clarified butter.

Harees requires a lengthy preparation. It has to be constantly stirred in order to avoid burning or sticking to the pot. It is, however, well worth the effort.

1 kg whole wheat grains
1 kg lamb meat with bones
¼ cup *dhen kheneen* (clarified butter or ghee)
salt to taste

Soak whole wheat in water overnight. Wash and pat dry lamb meat and bones. Put lamb meat, bones and salt in a large pot. Cover with water, bring to a boil, then simmer until almost cooked through. Drain soaked whole wheat and add to lamb meat. Cover pot and cook on low heat for 3–4 hours or until whole wheat has absorbed most of the liquid. Mix and check frequently.

You may have to add hot water in order to keep the *harees* moist and avoid sticking. Cook until lamb meat has separated from the bones and the *harees* is very smooth and elastic. Turn heat off. Remove and discard bones and fat.

To finish dish you have three options:

Option 1: Use a hand mixer and blend until the meat is dissolved into the wheat and has the consistency of cooked porridge.

Option 2: Use a wooden *harees* spoon called a *medhrab*, beat or whisk until the meat is dissolved into the wheat and has the consistency of cooked porridge.

Option 3: Use a large food mixer that resembles a 'cement mixer'. It is quick and very efficient and is often seen used by Emirati women who cook large amounts of *harees*.

Pour the *harees* into a large bowl and top with *dhen kheneen* or melted clarified butter. Serve while still warm.

Umm Mohammed explained that *harees* was traditionally served in a round coloured porcelain plate and enjoyed as a soothing comfort food.

Traditionally, Emirati families exercised a gifting food ritual before the sunset prayers that I still enjoy today. The exchange of legeimat amongst our neighbours and friends.

Rgaag

PAPER-THIN EMIRATI BREAD

SERVES 6–8

Rgaag is traditional, unleavened, paper thin bread that Emiratis enjoy eating for breakfast, lunch and dinner, and is also very popular during Ramadan. *Rgaag* is part of the *thareed* recipe family and can be eaten hot drizzled with oil and honey, date honey, eggs, herbs, ghee (clarified butter), cheese, zaatar, tomatoes, olives and spices.

The bread is made on a large circular iron plate called *tabi* and requires great skill to bake. The liquid bread dough is placed on the *tabi* over direct heat. The edges are carefully scraped using a spatula. It is then folded and served hot.

2 kg flour
1 tsp salt
2–3 cups water
1 bowl water for your hands
1 *tabi* (circular iron plate, can be bought at ethnic stores)
1 carpenter's spatula

Mix the flour and salt in a bowl and slowly add water to make semi-thick dough. The dough should be a thickness that allows it to be easily spread around the *tabi*. Cover with a kitchen towel and let rest for 30 minutes in a warm area. Place *tabi* on direct flame and when hot, spread a little oil over surface with paper towel. Dip your whole hand in water and take a handful of dough. Put dough on outer edge of *tabi*. Spread dough in circular fashion until it reaches the centre of the *tabi*. Holes can be quickly filled by dabbing dough on them. Leftover dough is dropped back into bowl. Use a carpenter's metal spatula to lift the bread once the edges are light brown and crisp. A steady hand will ensure that the *rgaag* doesn't break. Break 1 egg and/or use white cream cheese and spread all over dough. Continue cooking until egg is set or cheese has melted. Fold *rgaag* into triangles and serve while still hot.

Zaatar is the generic name for a family of related herbs of Middle Eastern origin i.e. oregano, basil and thyme.

NOORA ABDULRAHMAN ALMULLA ALZAROUNI
AL TAI, DUBAI

BEDOUIN HOSPITALITY AND BEDOUIN FOOD

Noora Al Zarouni is an impressive and intelligent young married woman and mother of six children. She is originally from Sharjah.

Noora works for the Dubai Health Authority and her husband Muhammad, an equally impressive individual, works for the Armed Forces of the United Arab Emirates in Dubai. Originally from Dubai, Muhammad was a well-known football player for the Dubai Club. He decided a long time ago to live his passion by running his own commercial and private animal farm in Al Tai, Dubai.

Both Noora and her husband own and run their large animal farm for commercial purposes as well as for their personal consumption. They have a beautifully reconstructed private 'heritage village' as I called it, situated right next to the animal farm.

Noora gave us a personal tour and in her gracious manner and grounded confidence described that their 'heritage village' included four Bedouin tents in different shapes and sizes. The tents were decorated with plaited mats or food trays known as *sarrut*, date baskets hooked on the walls, incense racks or *madkhanah* and pottery, used for their private gatherings and numerous large family functions.

With a soft voice she commented that she would prefer to have more functions at her villa in Dubai. However, their guests have grown accustomed to the hospitality of her family at the farm and 'heritage village'. Understandably so, my family and I experienced a lovely sense of peace and spaciousness while assisting in the cooking a young lamb from their animal farm which was slaughtered the day before.

The animal farm and their impressive Bedouin style 'heritage village' accommodating and honouring men and women in separate tents, are nestled between palm trees and surrounding farms.

My family and I sat on the floor or *sunnah*, as did the Prophet Mohammad, peace be upon him, for most of his daily activities. Today, Emiratis still follow this tradition which gives them a sense of being grounded and spreads a peaceful atmosphere amongst the family and their guests. 'Feeling grounded is a vital part of being together which creates trust amongst the members of the family and guests', commented Noora.

Noora went on to describe that once her guests arrive at their 'heritage village' she and her husband welcome them and invite them to sit on the floor, as this emphasizes the insignificance of their status while still enjoying the togetherness. Large platters laden with Arabic sweets and plenty of fruits staked on trays are always part of the welcoming repertoire. At this point I could sense Noora's enthusiasm in relaying her family's welcoming rituals! What a privilege I thought!

Noora impressed me with her knowledge of old Bedouin rituals: the *fualah* is one of the most important elements of welcoming rituals because that is the time when the host and hostess are able to observe their guests and judge their immediate needs as well as recognize signs that will indicate the duration of their guests' stay.

I personally had the privilege of experiencing the welcoming ritual which entailed catering to my needs as a guest. Without having to ask, Muhammad was aware that I desired more tea. He impressed me because he was able to multitask while he, with his children's assistance, prepared the fire for their favourite Bedouin meal, *ghouzy*.

Noora, while making sure that I was well attended to by her children, and in order to ensure that I was able to continue taking notes, went on to say, 'our guests love our exquisite Bedouin style lamb cooked by my husband, the children and me. After we have finished eating, we enjoy an evening of storytelling under the stars around a fire that always seems to have enough kindle and embers to last all night.'

The *fualah* ritual encompasses presenting and serving Emirati *qahwa* or coffee, tea, sweets, dates, bread, honey, fresh fruits, perfumes and incense. Noora's beautifully prepared *fualah* fuelled my curiosity. I had so many questions for my book that we agreed to defer them and enjoy our conversation in the moment! But while relishing the sweets laden with cream and nuts for dessert, I sat in a state of delightful silence.

We were only about 30 minutes away from the city of Dubai; still Noora and her family went out of their way to welcome us for the traditional *ghouzy*, normally served at lunch on special occasions. Traditionally, *ghouzy* is prepared by men, cooked over a low fire, and produced communally for their family and guests. This method allows the lamb's succulent juices to develop while it is being steamed inside the pot with hot embers on the lid and a fire under the pot.

While we were all sitting on the floor around the deliciously prepared lamb, the dish was giving off a savoury fragrance of mild spices in combination with the aromatic essence of the 'perfumed' basmati rice. To die for!

The dishes were accompanied by radish tails (*rowaid*), which is an essential green that was eaten by the Bedouins and is still part of the food repertoire amongst most Emiratis who consider radish tails to be a delicacy.

Muhammad made sure that we were shown the Emirati food ritual that he exercises with all his children: the experience of 'tactile eating'. Muhammad went on to say in English: 'This selection of food requires the ability to judge the texture, colour and smell of the food and products.'

The preparation and cooking of food will rely, as Muhammad stressed, on 'tactile contact' which is an essential part of the Emirati food culture and etiquette. He went on to say that tactile contact allows him to judge the temperature and quality of the dish being prepared and finally all members of the family and guests will eat with their hand; the right hand only!

Touching the food while eating is another subliminal way of acknowledging the food preparation and appreciating the food's texture by rolling it into a ball in the hand. Once rolled, the food is slowly and discreetly pushed with the thumb into the mouth while the four other fingers slowly curl back and the ball of food rests in the mouth without causing the fingers to become smothered with food.

At this point we had our plates filled with rice and topped with lamb and sauce, as well as some of the vegetables and radish tails on the side. Noora's family ate from a large dish, and each member of the family, eight of them, instinctually assigned themselves a space on the rice platter from which they would eat. In doing so, it allows them to rest without moving or usurping the space of the person seated on their left or right. It is also a sign of respect for the other guests. Order is thus maintained amongst the large number of adults and children eating from the same platter.

I was feeling an enormous amount of gratitude to be able to partake in the ceremony of 'eating under the sky', and for being taught how to eat in accordance with their etiquette. 'Tactile' and the 'mouthful' method of eating with the right hand was a very rewarding experience!

This was Noora's moment to take over, showing us how to eat 'the mouthful' or *logmah* in Arabic. Noora took rice, meat and a piece of vegetable into her right hand and slowly shaped it into a ball. She would 'massage' the food ball in her hand until she was ready to eat it. She then continued to explain that it was customary to draw pieces of meat towards you and then mix the torn pieces of meat with rice and small pieces of vegetables before raising the rolled food ball to the mouth. This is to honour the design of the meat in the centre of the circle of heaped rice and vegetables.

Her family and the children were all taught to take their 'mouthful', or *logmah*, from where they were seated which declares to all others that this is 'their area' from which they would be applying the brushing movements followed by shaping the food into a ball. This ritual or etiquette has a very practical reason behind it, namely order, hygiene, and respect for each other's food source.

After Noora and Muhammad had declared the end of the savoury meal, we were invited to return to the eating area of the tent next to the farm. This is when Muhammad announced that one of his sheep would be delivering two lambs and he asked us if we were interested in witnessing the birth of the 'twins'. I was so excited that I decided to take photographs of this double birthing event! What a privilege!

We were soon called to join the family for dessert. By this time, the afternoon had progressed to early evening and we devoured the Arabic sweets, especially Noora's homemade cake!

I thought to myself, how does Noora manage her family, farm, villa and career? In response Noora reflected that most of her children were independent and that her mother assisted her with her youngest child. She went on to say that a few months ago they had hired two housekeepers as well. With a smile she added that she would love to have more children! I admire Noora and her husband for their energy and managing skills!

After sharing a Bedouin day with Noora and her family, Mohammed drove us back over the dunes and gave us directions back to our car which we had left in the parking lot of Ikea in Dubai due to technical failure. We had hoped that the problem would be solved by the time we returned. And indeed as I turned the key in the ignition, the car started and we were on our way back to Abu Dhabi!

Bedouin Lamb Ghouzy is cooked in a pot over an open fire and served with rice.

Bedouin Lamb Ghouzy

LAMB STEW

SERVES 8–10

INGREDIENTS FOR LAMB:

1 small young lamb,5–6 kg
3 tbsp turmeric
3 tbsp black pepper powder
3 crushed *loumi* (dried lime, black in colour)
3 tbsp *bzar* (see page 15)
3 tbsp zaatar
3 tbsp red chilli powder
3 tbsp salt
4 cups yoghurt
3 large potatoes, peeled and cut into wedges
3 onions, peeled and cut into wedges
2 cans of fava beans or home cooked (4 cups)
3 large carrots, peeled and sliced

INGREDIENTS FOR RICE:

3 kg basmati rice
3 tbsp salt
water
coriander to garnish

Prepare the fire in sand with wood and charcoal. Bring to a low fire and prepare the embers which will be used during the last stage of cooking. These will be placed on top of the lid. Wash whole lamb and place it folded into a large basin. Cover with water for 3 hours.

Rinse and dry the lamb meat. Mix all the spices with the yoghurt and rub the mixture on the lamb inside and out. Place lamb into a bowl, cover and marinate in refrigerator overnight. Place marinated whole lamb on a rack inside a large pot. Carefully add water into the pot from the side until it barely touches lamb. Place all cut vegetables around. Cover. This method will steam the lamb and vegetables. Cook for approximately 2–3 hours. Check every 30 minutes and add water if necessary. You don't want the lamb to dry out and burn its juices.

After 2–3 hours test the meat for tenderness and when ready pour out the juice except one cup. Set juice aside and keep warm. Cover lamb with lid and place it back over the fire, making sure you now have embers and no flames under the pot. Place 4 cups of embers carefully on top of lid. Cook for approximately 30 minutes.

Soak rice 1 hour before lamb is finished cooking! Rinse basmati rice until water runs clear. Soak rice for 30 minutes in cold water. Drain. Cover with water. Add salt and bring to a boil. Reduce heat and simmer until rice is done. Remove rice from heat. Drain completely. Cover rice dish with lid to keep warm and set aside. Place lamb on a large platter. Serve with rice mounted on a separate platter. Garnish with coriander.

FATIMA ABDULLAH AHMED AL DHANHANI
DIBBA, FUJAIRAH

THE BEEKEEPER'S WIFE

Fatima, her husband and ten children live in Dibba, a settlement located between the mountains and the seacoast, northeast of the United Arab Emirates. Fatima and her husband are related and come from the same Al Dhanhani tribe.

When I arrived at Fatima's home, I was overwhelmed by the collection of archaeological artefacts in the courtyard. Fatima, gracious yet energetic, greeted me with three kisses on the same cheek indicating that I was accepted as her friend.

Fatima did not lose time. She explained that she enjoys collecting authentic archaeological pieces originating from Fujairah for their family's home museum in order to have the public appreciate the local history. The artefacts are scattered everywhere in Fatima's courtyard, backyard, even amongst her kitchen pots! The home museum, under construction while I was there, is next to their home and is a joint project between her and her husband.

Fatima impressed me: she teaches Emirati cooking to schoolgirls, a program supported by the government of Fujairah. She searches for more artefacts from Fujairah, and markets and sells their honey. Her husband is the owner of the Al Dhanhani Natural Honey company located in the Muhlab area in the mountains of Dibba while their honey preserve is not far from their home.

They own about four thousand bees imported from Egypt as well as many local Emirati bees which live in hives on sticks inside caves. The best, most exclusive, organic and expensive honey is made from the Emirati bees inside the caves!!! Their 'liquid gold' is sold to Emirati and international clients who pay 1,000 dirhams per kilogram (approximately 200 euros) for the cave honey and a little less for the box honey.

Time came to watch Fatima cook *machbous laham*, her favourite basmati rice-based dish with spices and lamb. She smiled and said: 'Alexandra, I prefer to cook our dishes outside in very large pots directly on burning wood collected from my farms. Cooking on slow burning fire fuses the flavours resulting in exquisite tasting food.' She started the fire in her courtyard and collected all ingredients including vegetables harvested from her farms.

All the women in the house were invited to come to the women's majlis (sitting room) to dip bread in the honey and homemade yoghurt drizzled with *dahnee*, or ghee. They were offered black tea or Emirati coffee infused with cardamom and saffron. The bread, yoghurt, tea and Emirati coffee were all made by Fatima herself! I realized that I was very privileged to be given the opportunity to taste the best honey in the Emirates.

The fire was ready so Fatima began her personal cooking show. She covered her face with a long black veil empowering her as the self-confident woman she is. Fatima's recipe and cooking methods come from her great-great-grandmother who belonged to the same Al Dhanhani tribe. Fatima claims that all women in her tribe are talented cooks who use the same cooking methods which always include the ritual of respect and acknowledgment of their female ancestors who through time passed on their talents and recipes to each new generation.

Fatima was right. Her flavourful dish enhanced by cooking directly on wood fire made it unforgettable. If you ever get a chance to visit her soon-to-be opened public museum you will be able to experience some of her passion for cooking, her homemade yoghurt, bread and honey from their preserve!

Bedouin machbous laham is a lamb stew cooked in a pot over an open fire and served with rice and baked sweet potatoes which were freshly harvested from Fatima's farm.

Bedouin Machbous Laham

LAMB STEW

SERVES 8–12

INGREDIENTS FOR LAMB:

1 small young lamb (5–6 kg)
8 onions, peeled and chopped
1 bell pepper, cut into cubes
3 tbsp turmeric powder
25 cardamom pods
5 soaked *loumi* (dried lime)
1 tbsp *bzar* (see page 15)
16 round red chilli peppers
25 garlic cloves, peeled
4 cups coriander, chopped
3 tbsp salt
15 large, sweet potatoes, unpeeled and wrapped in aluminium foil
ample date palm wood, fronds or any other types of firewood
large pot that will accommodate a lamb up to 10 kg

LAMB:

Prepare the fire in sand or in the backyard with firewood, date palm tree wood and fronds. Keep replenishing the fire with additional pieces of wood and prepare the embers that will be used during the last stage of cooking. Slaughter and skin a young lamb early in the morning. Wash until clean. Or buy 6 kg ready cut lamb at your favourite butcher. Request that the butcher give you the head and liver (in the Emirates and other Arab countries, both the head and liver are considered part of the 'welcoming the guest of honour' ritual). Cut lamb into 8 pieces. Keep the liver and the head intact. These will be served to the guest of honour. Skip this stage if you opted to buy ready cut lamb pieces.

Place lamb pieces in large basin. Cover with water and soak for 3 hours in a cool area. Rinse and dry the lamb. Place lamb and liver into a large pot that will accommodate a young lamb up to 10 kg. Fill pot with water covering the lamb, cover with a lid. Keep pot covered after each addition until the lamb is cooked. Cook lamb for 30 minutes, skimming surface regularly. Add onions, bell pepper and coriander, stir and cook for 10 minutes. Add chilli peppers, garlic and cardamom, stir and cook for 10 minutes. Add salt, turmeric and *bzar* (should be freshly roasted and ground shortly before adding it), stir and continue to cook. Add soaked *loumi*. Cook for another 1 to 1.5 hours. Check every 30 minutes and add water to cover lamb if necessary.

While meat is cooking rinse rice until water runs clean, leave to soak in cold water. When lamb is cooked, remove from pot, set aside, cover and keep warm. Remove 2 cups of the meat juice and set aside. Keep the rest of the meat juice inside the pot for the rice recipe. Place the sweet potatoes, which are wrapped in aluminium foil, on top of the hot embers under the pot. Bake sweet potatoes until soft, set aside and keep warm.

INGREDIENTS FOR RICE:

3 kg basmati rice

4 cups water

2 cups lamb juice (taken from the pot in which the lamb was cooked in)

1 cup Indian raisins, soaked

2 tbsp salt

1 tbsp ground cumin

3 tbsp *bzar* (see page 15)

½ cup vegetable oil

2 cups coriander, chopped, to garnish

RICE:

Soak rice 1 hour before lamb is finished cooking! Pour the pre-soaked rice into pot with the meat juice. Add 1 litre of water or enough to completely submerge rice in meat juice. Add soaked raisins, cumin and salt. Bring to a boil, then simmer for approximately 30 minutes or until cooked. Drain rice (keep drained liquid for other dishes, or feed it to your farm animals) and place rice back into the pot over the fire, simmer until the liquid is absorbed. Add *bzar* and oil to the rice, then add chopped coriander and gently toss. Stir rice until well mixed. Remove from fire. Spoon rice onto a large platter and top with lamb and the reserved meat juice. Place baked sweet potatoes (aluminium foil removed) around the platter. Garnish the *machbous* with coriander.

AZZA AL QUBAISI
ABU DHABI AND FUJAIRAH

RENOWNED AWARD WINNING EMIRATI ARTIST AND DESIGNER

In 2012, I visited the International Date Festival in Abu Dhabi. While there I was attracted to an exhibitor who created large-sized furniture made out of palm tree wood and stainless steel.

I was so impressed that I decided to sit on a one-meter palm tree trunk completely surrounded by pre-washed and polished palm tree branches. While sitting and enjoying dates and a demi-cup of cardamom Arabic coffee, a confident young Emirati woman presented herself to me exclaiming: 'I am artist Azza Al Qubaisi.'

She kindly asked if I wanted to be photographed while sitting on one of her pieces of art. What a born diplomat, I thought! Azza took a photo of me before I had time to answer. As we were conversing I told her that I had seldom sat in such a comfortable chair. I reflected that this must be a perfectly balanced piece of art/chair which could be classified as 'ergonomic'.

Azza went on to explain that she had been interested in 'natural materials' since her childhood and that she would work parallel with the natural laws in order to create pieces of art. Azza maintained that it was of vital importance that she create products that respect the laws of 'natural wastes' which in turn became comfortable and practical for the user while never forcing the user to 'fit' her creations.

Azza then decided to show me her unique silver jewellery which to my amazement reflected an advanced level of natural talents and which captured the culture and spirit of the United Arab Emirates. This was exactly what I was looking for! I was so impressed that I bought three pairs of silver cufflinks depicting a *ghutrah* which is a typical headscarf worn by Emirati men.

Azza was born in the capital Abu Dhabi which is in the southwest of the United Arab Emirates. She hails from a tribe of the same name, 'Al Qubaisi' in Liwa, a large oasis approximately 225 km away from Abu Dhabi. When Azza describes her tribal place of origin she smiles with a reminiscent look and goes on to describe the beauty of the Oasis, also known for one of the world's largest and tallest sand dunes in the United Arab Emirates.

Educated in London, she studied at Chelsea College of Art, and obtained her BA in silversmithing, jewellery and allied crafts from the London Guildhall University and the HRD Institute of Gemology in Antwerp, Belgium. In addition, Azza has an MA in creative and cultural industries from HCT-CERT in Abu Dhabi.

Azza is without a doubt an artist of diverse talent who discovered that becoming an entrepreneur was important in order to ensure that the population of her home country, as well as buyers abroad, would enjoy her creations reflecting the culture of the United Arab Emirates. Azza is a natural ambassador for her distinctive artistic creations which so many have had the good fortune to acquire.

Azza established her own brand 'The Arabian Workshop for Jewellery and Gemstones' (ARJMST) in 2003, designing and producing exceptional jewellery collections and distinctive customized pieces. I personally enjoyed participating in a number of her 'out of the ordinary' workshops which include preparing the design through a cuttlefish bone casting technique, a fascinating method of carving one's personal creations onto the cuttlefish bone. In the casting process the cuttlefish mould is destroyed, thus resulting in each piece becoming an individual and unique piece of art.

Just before leaving, Azza casually told me that she is the first artist to design and produce Emirati corporate gifts and trophies, creating original and unique pieces for each client. She designed the awards which were given out for the 'Million's Poet', a competition for the most talented poet in Arabic poetry, at HH Sheikh Mansoor Bin Zayed Al Nahyan Global Arabian Horse Flat Racing Festival.

We continued talking and I learned that Azza teaches jewellery making in the United Arab Emirates and that she established a Non Governmental Organization (NGO) project in 2006 to encourage, motivate, develop and promote local handicrafts with the label 'made in the United Arab Emirates'. As a volunteer, Azza also developed and promoted two governmental handicraft projects. Some of Azza's handicrafts are created by local Emiratis in Abu Dhabi. In addition, Azza has created and launched a designer incubator (organization) in Madinat Zayed City in the Western region of Abu Dhabi.

Azza Al Qubaisi coaches a group of nine passionate United Arab Emirates jewel designers to become graduate jewellery designers. She received numerous awards of excellence on behalf of the United Arab Emirates. Her artworks are regularly shown in solo and group exhibitions, public shows and festivals around the Emirates. Azza is a consistent award winning artist whose creations represent the present and future in design while being respectful of Emirati tradition and preventing their values from being forgotten.

I had lost contact with Azza for about three years when a friend of mine recommended that I contact Azza to interview her for my Emirati Cookbook. This is when Azza decided spontaneously to invite me to visit the coastal city of Fujairah, located on the Gulf of Oman, where she is creating public art inspired by local natural materials. I was touched by her hospitality and kindness which she has displayed throughout our friendship. While her husband drove us to Fujairah, I learned that it was her father who encouraged her to become a student in England and pursue a career following her passion for the arts.

When we arrived in Fujairah, the fifth largest Emirate of the United Arab Emirates and the only Emirate that has a coastline along the Gulf of Oman (and none on the Arabian Gulf), Azza went on to relay that her workshop is a place of refuge, relaxation and inspiration which stimulates her artistic creativity. I could not help but notice that the front and rear walls of her workshop were covered with carefully bundled palm tree branches that were prepared, washed and polished on her father's farm in Liwa.

Azza considers the date palm tree to be one of the most beautiful gifts given by Allah and an important resource to the people living in the United Arab Emirates. It provides the population with dates, syrup, sugar, coffee and excellent quality fibre from which Azza draws so much enjoyment when creating her favourite pieces of functional art which she branded 'Yareda'. Her personally designed palm tree functional art seems to market quickly, especially within the international community.

Azza creates from her soul and is truly a gifted person who never ceases to amaze me with her boundless energy and her never-ending inspiration no matter where she is. Early in the morning, she can be seen walking along the seashore collecting seashells, fish skins drying in the sun, pebbles, beach stones, palm tree trunks and driftwood washed up from the ocean which she beautifully and artistically organizes.

Azza, who is a vegetarian, agreed to cook from the local cuisine inspired by one of her neighbours in the Qidfa district of Fujairah. Her talents seem to extend straight to the kitchen as well. Azza amazed me when she agreed to be interviewed for my traditional Emirati cookbook.

Azza, her husband and their two children took me to her favourite vegetable, fruit and fish market in Fujairah where the food is as diverse as its inhabitants while remaining authentic.

Azza was eager to cook some of the little known dishes that continue to be cooked by the Bedouins living in Fujairah. I had the privilege of being introduced to two kind elder Bedouins who were obviously enjoying their tea and mangoes while seated and chatting quietly on the sidewalk in front of the workshop. Both ladies remained firm in not allowing me to take photographs of them. Nonetheless, they invited me to join them in their Arabic coffee ritual.

Imagine! Sitting on a sidewalk along a dirt road, sipping cardamom and ginger tea and chatting with two Bedouin women as if we were sitting in a living room! What memorable moments!

I know that you will not only enjoy Azza's traditional Fujairah recipes but you will also be moved by her enthusiasm as you browse through photos I captured of her while cooking!

Bedouin Sehnah with Rice

DRIED SARDINES WITH RICE

SERVES 4–6

Sehnah is a popular Fujairah condiment produced with dried sardines. These can be seen drying on sand and sometimes on empty side roads. *Sehnah* is added on rice or other dishes to impart a flavour of sun-dried sardines.

INGREDIENTS FOR RICE:

2 cups basmati rice
8 cups cold water
1 tsp salt
3 green cardamom pods, cracked
½ tsp whole black peppercorns

INGREDIENTS FOR SEHNAH:

2 cups whole *sehnah* or dried sardines
½ tsp fennel seeds, toasted

INGREDIENTS FOR TOPPING OF RICE DISH:

1 cup coriander, finely chopped
1 cup *sehnah*
4–6 whole sardines, toasted or untoasted

RICE:

Rinse basmati rice until water runs clear. Soak rice for 30 minutes in cold water. Drain. Add all ingredients to water and bring to a boil. Simmer until rice is cooked. Cover with lid, keep warm and set aside.

SEHNAH:

In a small frying pan gently dry-fry fennel seeds on medium heat. Fennel seeds will darken in colour and they will pop. When you smell the fragrant seeds, they are done! Take a mortar and pestle (or small food processor) and grind sardines with the toasted fennel seeds.

TOPPING:

Sprinkle *sehnah* over rice. Garnish with coriander.

Optional: You may wish to toast whole sardines in a frying pan (without oil) on low heat until you are able to smell the sardines toasting. This takes only a few minutes. Remove from heat and cool. Decorate rice with toasted whole sardines. This *sehnah* or dried sardines on rice is extraordinarily healthy, easy to make, and delicious!

Bedouin Clams, Mussels and Spicy Tomato Sauce

SERVES 4–6

INGREDIENTS FOR RICE:

2 cups basmati rice
8 cup cold water
1 tsp salt
3 green cardamom pods
½ tsp whole black peppercorns

INGREDIENTS FOR MUSSELS:

2 kg mussels
2 medium onions, peeled and minced
3 garlic cloves, peeled and minced
3 cups water
2 tsp salt

INGREDIENTS FOR CLAMS:

2 kg fresh clams
2 medium onions, peeled and minced
3 garlic cloves, peeled and minced
3 cups water
2 tsp salt

RICE:

Rinse basmati rice until water runs clear. Soak rice for 30 minutes in cold water. Drain. Add all ingredients to water and bring to a boil. Simmer until rice is cooked. Remove from heat, drain completely. Cover with lid, keep warm and set aside.

MUSSELS:

When buying mussels, look for those with tightly closed shells which smell fresh! Discard mussels that remain open when tapped with fingers or against the kitchen counter. Scrub mussels under cold running water. De-beard mussels. You may want to use a pair of tweezers. In large pot add water, mussels, salt, minced onion and garlic. Cover and cook on medium heat for 5 minutes. Shake pot while cooking to ensure even cooking of mussels. After 5 minutes remove lid. All mussels should be open. If not, cover and cook an additional 3 minutes. Discard any mussels that have not opened! Remove mussels with slotted spoon and set aside until cool enough to remove the mussels from their shells. Place the mussels without the shells into a medium sized serving bowl. Cover with tea towel and set aside.

CLAMS:

Discard any clams that are broken, chipped or remain open when tapped against the kitchen counter. Fill a large pot with 2–3 litres of fresh water. Add clams and soak, submerged, for 30 minutes. Cover with tea towel and place in refrigerator. After 30 minutes, clams will have naturally released most of the salt, sand and any other ocean particles. Scrub clams under cold running water. Take a large pot and add water, clams, salt, minced onion, and garlic. Bring to a boil, reduce heat, cover and cook for 3–4 minutes until clams open. Shake pot while cooking to ensure even cooking of clams. Avoid overcooking as they will lose their tenderness. Remove clams with a slotted spoon and set aside until cool enough to remove from their shells. Shell clams, place in bowl and set aside.

INGREDIENTS FOR SPICY TOMATO SAUCE:

3 tbsp vegetable oil
2 large onions, peeled and finely chopped
6 garlic cloves, peeled and minced
1 cup tomatoes, crushed
4 tbsp tomato concentrate
¼ tsp red pepper
1 ½ tsp cumin powder
1 tsp salt or to taste
black pepper to taste
1 ½ cups water

GARNISH:

½ cup fresh coriander, chopped
4 lime wedges

SPICY TOMATO SAUCE:

Heat oil in large, heavy saucepan over medium heat, add onion, garlic and crushed red pepper. Stir and cook until onion is translucent. Add remaining ingredients, bring to boil slowly. Simmer for 30 minutes or until sauce thickens.

FINAL STEP:

Transfer mussels and clams into tomato sauce. Stir and simmer for about 2–3 minutes. Remove sauce from heat and transfer to a serving dish. Sprinkle with chopped coriander and garnish with lime wedges. Serve over rice.

This dish is highly valued in the Fujairah Bedouin Cuisine!

NAJAT SAYED AL HASHEMI
DUBAI

FOOD AND LIFE MUST BE IN HARMONY

This is the inspiring story of Najat Sayed Al Hashemi, a tall and energetic woman in her early fifties. I was introduced to Najat Sayed Al Hashemi through her friend Heyam Hassan. Heyam sold me a designer frame consisting of three beautifully crafted Emirati *burqas*, also known as masks, often seen on elder women from the Emirates who wear *burqas* on a daily basis as a matter of tradition.

Najat is an academic of noble background, she is a mother of three who runs her own beauty salon in Dubai. Her sparkling eyes reflect her innate curiosity!

She has a strong attachment to what is natural and organic, and she views the world with respect. She emphasizes that Allah the Creator has gifted us with beauty and harmony from which we can all learn.

Her father, Sayed Mohammed Youssef, is from the Hashemi tribe in Iran and is a direct descendant of Prophet Muhammad. Her maternal Emirati grandfather was an academic who worked in the late 1930's for Sheikh Shahmoud. He won an award of recognition for his esteemed services in the Government of Abu Dhabi. Her Emirati mother is also an academic and raised her own children. Najat recalls that her childhood was filled with love, kindness and affection: 'I am very grateful to my parents who dedicated their lives ensuring that all their children became academics.'

While interviewing Najat, I realized that one of her numerous passions is cooking traditional Emirati dishes with a distinct touch of innovation. 'Emirati traditional food is inventive, rich, healthy and colourful,' explained Najat. 'The good balance in the amount and variety of spices helps to achieve a harmony in taste, flavour and colours in accordance with one's taste.'

Najat proudly continued: 'Traditional Emirati dishes have evolved from and are strongly influenced by Persian and Indian cuisine, thus creating a "Perso–Indian Fusion Cuisine" of exotic yet simple dishes. The Indians enriched Emirati cuisine with their blend of spices.'

Emirati dishes are similar to Persian ones in that they are based on rice with meat, chicken or fish with vegetables. Whereas Persian cuisine is not spicy, it introduced the saffron. Persian saffron has a distinctly gentle, elegant fragrance and flavour. It differs from its Spanish counterpart. Persian organic saffron threads are stamens of the crocus flowers and are the most expensive spice on earth. 'Iranian saffron is my top choice. You must make sure that it is organic and that you smell the saffron before buying it. Sometimes saffron smells elegantly woody with a hint of walnut and sometimes the spice expresses a fragrance of musk and walnut with a floral hint,' confided Najat. The Persian homegrown saffron is often mixed with a little sugar and pounded in a mortar and pestle to which hot water is added. Dishes are garnished with this mixture.

I witnessed Najat's love and passion in the preparation of the *tahta* dish, one version with chicken and the other without. After eating, Najat took me on a tour of her beauty salon located in her former family home and converted into a beauty salon and day spa getaway. Her warm-hearted staff ensured that I was welcomed in the traditional Emirati fashion: first water then tea followed by dainty biscuits. One of the staff members said: 'You deserve to be pampered.' And indeed I was!

Our farewell involved the ritual of the hostess sprinkling the guest with an array of oils and perfumes. Najat exclaimed: 'You will remember me by this unique homemade perfume and oil mixture.' She then sprayed it on my clothes. Najat is so very innovative and great fun to be with!

In Arabic dajaj means 'chicken' and tahta means 'under', therefore, the chicken is under the rice!

Tahta Dajaj

CHICKEN WITH RICE

SERVES 4–6

INGREDIENTS FOR DAJAJ:

1 kg chicken, cut into pieces
4 tbsp oil
1 large onion, peeled and diced
4 large tomatoes, diced
2 tsp turmeric powder
3 *loumi* (dried lime)
1 tsp *bzar* (see page 15)
½ tsp cinnamon powder
2 tsp sea salt
½ tsp pepper, ground
2–4 tbsp water (if required)

INGREDIENTS FOR RICE:

4 cups rice
1 tsp sea salt
water
10 saffron threads
½ cup coriander, chopped (optional)

Rinse rice and drain. Place rice in bowl and cover with water. Soak until you are ready to cook. Use mortar and pestle and grind 10 saffron threads. Pour 3 tbsp hot water, mix, cover and set aside. In large skillet, heat vegetable oil at medium heat and fry onion until translucent. Add turmeric, stir for 30 seconds only to avoid burning it. Add *bzar* or Emirati spice and keep stirring. Do not add more oil! Use mortar and pestle to crack *loumi*, remove hard peel and seeds. Add what is left to the mixture. Add diced tomatoes, stir, bring to a boil, cover and simmer over very low heat for approximately 5 minutes. If mixture begins to stick add a little water, 1 tbsp at a time. Add chicken pieces, stir and cover. Leave on medium-low heat for 15 minutes or until half cooked. Remove lid and simmer for another 15 minutes or until approximately 75% of the liquid has evaporated. Check chicken for doneness. Add salt, pepper and cinnamon, stir, cover and set aside. Boil 4 litres of water. Add drained rice and salt to boiling water. Cook rice over medium heat until half cooked. Remove rice from heat, drain in a colander and place on top of the chicken mixture. Cover and cook over low heat for 20 minutes or until rice is fluffy and ready to eat. Serve on a large platter. Drizzle liquid saffron over rice for visual effect and flavour. Garnish with chopped coriander. Serve *tahta dajaj* while hot!

Najat's *tahta dajaj*, or Chicken with Rice, is a traditional Emirati recipe given to her by her mother. It's cooked with very little oil and yet is very flavourful. Traditional recipes always evolve, and this one has evolved using very little oil.

Tahta Khodhar

VEGETABLES WITH RICE

SERVES 4–6

INGREDIENTS FOR KHODAR:

2 tbsp oil
2 tbsp butter
2 tbsp butter for mushrooms
1 large onion, peeled and diced
2 large tomatoes, diced
2 large zucchinis, diced
¼ kg fresh champignons mushrooms
¼ kg fresh green beans
1 tsp turmeric powder
2 *loumi* (dried lime)
1 tsp *bzar* (see page 15)
½ tsp cinnamon powder
½ cup coriander, chopped
½ cup parsley, chopped
2 tsp sea salt
½ tsp pepper, ground

INGREDIENTS FOR RICE:

4 cups rice
1 tsp sea salt
water
10 saffron threads

Rinse rice and drain. Place rice in bowl and cover with water. Soak rice until you are ready to cook. Rinse, trim and cut green beans into 4 cm pieces. Cover and set aside. Rinse, trim, and cut mushrooms into 4 pieces. Cover and set aside. Use mortar and pestle to grind 10 saffron threads. Add 3 tbsp hot water, mix, cover and set aside.Use mortar and pestle to crack *loumi*. Remove hard peel and seeds. Set aside. In large skillet, melt 2 tbsp butter over medium heat. Sauté mushrooms until tender, cover and set aside. In large skillet, heat vegetable oil and 2 tbsp of butter at medium heat and fry onion until it appears translucent. Add turmeric and stir for 30 seconds. Add *bzar* or Emirati spice and keep stirring. Do not add more oil! Add cleaned *loumi*, tomatoes, zucchini and beans and keep stirring at medium-low heat for approximately 30 minutes. Cover. Stir regularly to avoid sticking. If liquid is needed, add 1–5 tbsp of water, one tbsp at a time. After 15 minutes, remove lid, stir and simmer until approximately 75% of liquid has evaporated. Add sautéed mushrooms, stir and simmer for another 5 minutes. Season with salt and pepper. Add coriander, parsley and cinnamon, and stir gently. Turn heat off, cover and set aside. Boil 4 litres of water. Add drained rice and salt to boiling water. Cook rice over medium heat until half cooked. Remove rice from heat, drain in a colander and place on top of the vegetable mixture. Cover and cook over low heat for 20 minutes, or until the rice is fluffy and ready to eat. Transfer *tahta khodhar* onto a large serving platter and drizzle liquid saffron over rice for visual effect and flavour. Serve while hot!

Najat's *tahta khodar*, or vegetables with rice, is also based on her mother's traditional Emirati recipe.

SALHA AL SHAMSI
AL AIN

A LEADING EMIRATI KITCHEN AND RESTAURANT RUN BY AN EMIRATI WOMAN

Salha Al Shamsi welcomed me attired in a stunning black lace *abaya*, her penetrating black eyes accentuated by a double veil hijab. Hailing from the tribe of the same name, Salha is in charge of one of the most authentic Emirati kitchens in Al Ain. Al Ajdad Local Cusiene ('Cusiene' spelled correctly ie 'cuisine' means 'kitchen' in French) was originally owned by a Jordanian who sold the premises to Salha in 2007. She decided to keep the name with the 'minor' spelling error because despite it, the restaurant had a well-established and loyal clientele from across the United Arab Emirates.

Al Ajdad Local Cusiene is a large restaurant and kitchen nestled in sun bathed, picturesque Al Ain, two hours from Abu Dhabi. Her business has taken off! She uses only high quality, fresh products which makes an appealing difference when producing her authentic Emirati dishes. Some of her dishes have a hint of certain spices that are not found at other Emirati restaurants.

Salha obtained a Bachelor's degree in Political Science from the United Arab Emirates University in Al Ain. Upon her return from a holiday in Garmisch Patenkirchen, southern Germany, Salha decided to follow her passion of becoming an entrepreneur, and in 2007 bought the kitchen and restaurant.

Her goal is to develop the most authentic Emirati kitchen in the United Arab Emirates. Salha's philosophy is to cook only freshly prepared dishes for her customers who order from her fualah list which she entitles her 'Royal *Fualah* Dishes'. According to Salha, breakfast and supper are considered minor meals in the United Arab Emirates while lunch and *fualah* are the most important. *Fualah* is a ritual which includes food, coffee, perfumes and incense served between meals.

Following are Salha's favourite 'Royal *Fualah* Dishes' from the menu based on her family's traditional recipes passed on from generation to generation:

Chbaab: similar to a thin, round pancake.
Khameer: round, flat yeast bread.
Legeimat: similar to miniature-sized, plain doughnuts.
Khanfaroush: a large version of a flat, round legeimat with the addition of eggs.
Aseeda: the appearance of a crème caramel but with the addition of saffron and rose water.
Khabees: mix of flour and oil resulting in large-sized clusters with grainy-like consistency.
Mochalla: similar to pancakes folded twice.
Gors with dates: bread baked with dates.
Gors with sugar: bread sprinkled with sugar.
Harees: similar to porridge but made from whole wheat grains.
Margooga: a meat or chicken stew with soft bread strips.
Balaleet: sweet Asian vermicelli noodles with eggs with saffron.

I had the privilege of tasting a few and was struck by the freshness and the balanced blend of spices in every dish. I also noticed the three essential non-visual categories which were respected: temperature, taste and texture of the dishes.

For example, with my favourite dish *margooga*, the dish temperature was indeed hot, but not so hot that it would burn my tongue. The taste was mild, with a perfectly balanced mix of cloves, dried lime, pepper, cardamom, turmeric and *bzar* (Emirati spice mix). The texture of the *margooga* was pudding-like but each bite had a piece of 'stirred bread', softly cooked potatoes and tender chicken. The Emirati homemade butter carried the flavour directly to the 'heart'. No doubt I was in 'taste heaven'.

Margooga

DELUXE CHICKEN STEW WITH BREAD DOUGH

SERVES 6–8

INGREDIENTS FOR MARGOOGA:

1 kg whole chicken cut into 8–10 pieces
⅓ cup vegetable oil
2 onions, peeled and diced
1 large potato, peeled and cubed
3 medium carrots, peeled and sliced
3 large tomatoes, diced
1 *loumi* (dried lime), crushed
1 tbsp salt
½ tsp chilli powder
1 tsp ginger, crushed
½ tsp saffron threads
1 tbsp garlic cloves peeled and crushed
2 tbsp *bzar* (see page 15)
1 cup coriander, chopped, to garnish

INGREDIENTS FOR BREAD:

3 cups white flour
½ tsp salt
¾–1 cup lukewarm water

MARGOOGA

Rub chicken with ½ tsp *bzar* and leave for 30 minutes in refrigerator or until ready to cook. Fry onions in oil until transparent. Add the rest of the *bzar*, garlic, ginger, chilli, and cook until spices become fragrant. Add chicken and cook over moderate heat until chicken begins to colour. Add tomatoes, *loumi*, ½ cup of water and saffron and mix well over moderate heat. Cover pan and cook until spices become fragrant. Add cubed / sliced vegetables, 6 cups of water and salt, stir well and bring to a boil. Cover and simmer until water is reduced by half and chicken and vegetables are cooked. Carefully drop soft bread squares into hot chicken stew and stir slowly until thickened. Remove from heat and leave covered for 5 minutes. Garnish with chopped coriander.

BREAD

Put flour and add salt in a bowl. Slowly add lukewarm water and stir. Knead and mix with your fingers until the dough becomes smooth and elastic. Roll gently on a floured surface. The dough should reach a thickness of about ¼ cm. Cover with a tea towel and leave the dough to dry. This process may take a few hours. Dough should be dry on the surface. Cut dried dough in 4 cm x 4 cm squares. This bread for *margooga* stays unbaked.

Emirati clarified spiced butter is similar to ghee, very easy to make, and in the process the clarified butter becomes rich, creamy and slightly sweet.

Dhen Kheneen

EMIRATI CLARIFIED BUTTER

YIELDS: 1 CUP

2 cups unsalted butter
2 tbsp white flour
2 tbsp *bzar* (see page 15)
1 mesh strainer lined with 2 layers of cheesecloth over a heat-proof recipient to prepare ahead of time.

Lightly roast *bzar* in a dry frying pan and allow to cool. Place butter in heavy saucepan over low heat and melt. Add flour and *bzar* and stir slowly for approximately 3 minutes. Remove froth with a spoon and continue removing until there is no more froth and the butter is clear on the surface while flour and spices remain at the bottom of the pan. This process may take approximately 25 minutes (do not allow the froth to rise to the top of the pan as it may boil over). Carefully pour warm butter through the cheesecloth-lined strainer into recipient and discard the solids. Strain as often as necessary or until butter is clear. Cool.

Clarified butter can be stored in a sealed container for up to one month or longer if frozen.

Homemade Butter

Homemade Emirati butter is simple to make and is an exquisite taste enhancer. 1 cup of cream will yield approximately ½ cup butter and ½ cup buttermilk.

1 cup 35% heavy cream
1 pinch salt (optional)

Pour cream into a food processor and blend at medium speed. Process until butter separates and becomes a ball of butter. This process may take up to 10 minutes. Strain off buttermilk. Add salt if required. Refrigerate to keep the butter fresh. The extracted buttermilk can be used for drinking, baking and cooking.

This balaleet recipe deserves an award. It's a simple dish with an unexpected but elegant taste and aroma!

Balaleet

SWEET RICE VERMICELLI WITH EGGS AND ONION

SERVES 6–8

200 g rice vermicelli
1 small onion, peeled and thinly sliced
¼ cup sugar
½ tsp saffron threads
⅓ cup clarified butter (or homemade Emirati butter)
1 tsp cardamom powder
½ tsp curry powder
1 tsp rose water
¼ cup whole almonds, roasted
¼ cup raisins
3 eggs, lightly beaten
salt to taste

Boil water in large pot, add rice vermicelli and cook for 3 minutes. Drain and transfer to large bowl. Add sugar and carefully toss until sugar has dissolved completely. Add rose-water, saffron and cardamom powder and mix gently. Cover pot with a lid wrapped in a tea towel. This will absorb the excess liquid while the mixture is kept warm. Heat butter in a pan over medium heat and fry onion until lightly coloured. Add curry and salt. Add eggs and gently stir until eggs are cooked. Place egg mixture over noodles. Top with roasted almonds and raisins.

Mohalla

EMIRATI WHOLE WHEAT PANCAKE

YIELD: 1 DOZEN DEPENDING ON SIZE

2¼ cups whole wheat flour
1¼ cups powdered milk
4 eggs
½ tsp saffron powder
4 cups water (or as needed to create a smooth, fluid dough)
vegetable oil for frying
12 tsp Emirati butter
12 tsp *bzar* (see page 15)
12 tsp sugar

In large mixing bowl whisk together flour, saffron, powdered milk and eggs. Gradually add water and whisk until there are no lumps, dough is smooth and has become liquid in consistency. Allow batter to rest for 1 hour. Stir batter before making the *mohalla*. Heat 1 teaspoon of vegetable oil in frying pan over medium to high heat. Pour a thin layer of batter in pan and quickly spread in a circular motion coating the surface evenly. Cook until bottom has become medium amber colour. Transfer cooked *mohalla* to platter and keep warm in slow oven while you cook the rest of the batter. Brush homemade Emirati butter mixed with *bzar* over each *mohalla*, then fold into triangle. Sprinkle with sugar. Before serving, sprinkle 1 teaspoon of sugar on each pancake.

Khanfaroush

3-BITER THICK FRIED PANCAKE

YIELD: 2 DOZEN DEPENDING ON SIZE

This recipe is very similar to the traditional *legeimat* but with the addition of 3 eggs which make the *khanfaroush* smoother and fluffier. This is an exquisite sweet treat!

1½ cups white flour
½ cup powdered milk
1 cup yoghurt
3 eggs, beaten
1 tbsp instant yeast
½ tsp saffron powder
¼ cup sugar
½ tsp salt
½–¾ cup water (or as needed to create liquid dough)
3 cups oil for frying
¼ cup date syrup to garnish

Using your hands, mix all dry ingredients in large bowl until there are no lumps. Mix yoghurt and eggs. Add to dry ingredients along with water and knead, alternately slapping dough against the side of bowl until dough is smooth and has become slightly liquid in consistency. This method of slapping against the bowl is to make sure there are no lumps. Allow dough to rest for approximately 30 minutes, or until dough has doubled in volume. Heat oil in a deep pan over a medium heat. Using your thumb, index and middle fingers lift dough to create medium sized balls equivalent to 2 large tablespoons. Fry them in hot oil. Turn *khanfaroush* using a large metal spoon to get an even golden colour. Dip your fingers in water in between each *khanfaroush*. Once *khanfaroush* are ready, transfer to a large bowl .Pour date syrup over and carefully mix before serving. Best eaten while still warm.

FATIMA AL GHUFLI
AJMAN

THE AWARD WINNING FOOD COMPETITION BEDOUIN FAMILY OF AJMAN

I am forever grateful to Amal Obaid Al Mazrouie for having arranged two interviews with her family in Ajman. I visited two well-known Bedouin families who still live very much as they have for the past forty years. This chapter will describe my first interview with Amal's family.

My daughter Tamara and I drove to Ajman to interview Fatima Al Ghufli. Sheikha, Fatima's daughter, welcomed us with open arms and agreed to be my translator and guide for the day. Khalifa, Fatima's son, proudly told me that he, his mother and father Saif had won the coveted Chef's award during the 2013 / 14 'Dubai World Hospitality Championships'.

Fatima introduced herself stating: 'Alexandra, I am a modern Emirati Bedouin whose family came from the Al Mazrouie tribe in Al Ain, in the Emirate of Abu Dhabi. With time, most of our families moved to Ajman and across the United Arab Emirates. Our main source of income was from agriculture and animal herding. Today, I still herd camels and sheep.'

Fatima explained that her family's tribal traditions and etiquette are still being followed every day. The younger generations are educated to become part of the strong 'Emiratization' employment initiative in the United Arab Emirates. She continued on: 'The patriarchal order plays a strong traditional role but is consciously adjusted and adapted to our modern way of life. More educated women are entering the workforce. The woman's income is considered and accepted as her money. If she marries, it is the husband's responsibility to earn income for himself and for his family.'

While quietly sipping her Emirati home cooked coffee she said: 'Our children are a reflection of our souls and they are never segregated or separated, in fact they participate in our lives and they learn the meaning of becoming a 'family team player'. Thus leadership foundations are developed and established.

Our elders are cared for in our homes because we prefer that they die at home amongst the family members. We have our own social security since every person in the family plays an important role in building and maintaining a strong foundation of loyalty. We know that we have a strong moral support system as well as support from our government. Thus every Emirati family bases its foundation on the same or similar cultural and social principles.

I am a grandmother and my generation is well versed in the old Bedouin cultures. One of my many tasks is to teach the younger generation how to revive their understanding of our traditional food and food etiquette culture. The rewards are immeasurable.'

For the interviews we gathered several times a day to sit on the floor, sipping tea, coffee, juices, water or chai. The first gathering was shortly after our arrival at 10 am followed by a light *fualah*. Two hours later Fatima served us a traditional Emirati lunch: Bedouin fish and rice, a fish stew, and white rice cooked with spices.

Then Fatima prepared *balaleet*, her favourite dinner dish which is a combination of thin rice noodles cooked with sugar, onions, cinnamon and ghee-fried omelette. I also received her favourite Emirati Bedouin Coffee recipe.

It was now 8 pm and to our surprise, Fatima sprinkled us with her mix of different oils and perfumes, a hospitality ritual but also a sign that the guests are ready to go. I felt truly blessed for having been afforded such a marvellous experience.

Bedouin Sherry Fish Stew with Rice

SERVES 10–12

INGREDIENTS FOR SHERRY FISH:

4–5 medium sherry fish
4 tbsp turmeric powder
2 tbsp salt
5 large tomatoes, cubed
2 large green peppers (capsicum)
5 *loumi* (dried limes)
250 g tamarind, soaked in 1 litre water for 10 minutes
6 tbsp lemon juice
3 garlic bulbs, peeled and chopped
2 tsp cardamom pods
500 g Indian squash (or any squash), cubed
salt (optional)
2 cups coriander, chopped, to garnish

INGREDIENTS FOR RICE:

4 cups good quality basmati rice
16 cups cold water
2 tsp salt
6 green cardamom pods
1 tsp whole black peppercorns

Clean and rinse fish with salt until water runs clean. Remove intestines, tail, gills and eggs. Slice fish into several pieces. Coat the fish with salt and turmeric. In a pot big enough to accommodate the fish, dry-roast cardamom on low heat for 1 minute. Stir continuously to prevent cardamom from burning. Increase heat to medium, add fish, cubed tomatoes, green peppers and *loumi*. Cover. Gently shake pot back and forth, cook for 3 minutes. In the meantime, strain soaked tamarind making sure you are left with a smooth tamarind paste. Set aside. Add the strained tamarind, 5 cups of boiling water, lemon juice and crushed garlic. Gently mix fish mixture, cover and cook on medium heat for 5 minutes. Add 2 litres of water and add squash. Cook until done. Taste for flavour and adjust with salt if necessary. Cover, set aside until rice is cooked.

RICE:

Rinse basmati rice until water runs clear. Soak for 30 minutes in cold water. Drain. In large pot, bring water to a boil. Add all ingredients. Simmer until rice is cooked. Remove rice from heat, drain well. Cover, keep warm and set aside. To serve, gently place sherry fish and vegetables on rice and garnish with chopped coriander.

Truly an exquisite Bedouin fish dish to enjoy any day of the week!

Semach Magli with Rice

FRIED FISH WITH RICE

SERVES 12–16

5 kg fish of your choice
4 tbsp salt
4 tbsp turmeric powder
4 tbsp fresh lemon juice
10 onions, peeled and chopped
5 tbsp oil or Emirati clarified butter or ghee
3 tbsp garlic cloves, peeled and chopped
3 tbsp ginger, peeled and mashed
3 tbsp *bzar* (see page 15)
1 cup coriander, chopped

INGREDIENTS FOR RICE:

2 cups good quality basmati rice
8 cups cold water
1 tsp salt
3 green cardamom pods
½ tsp whole black peppercorns

Clean and rinse fish with salt until water runs clean. Remove intestines, tail, gills and eggs. Coat the fish with salt, turmeric, *bzar* and lemon and leave to marinate for 15 minutes. In deep pan large enough to accommodate fish, dry-roast onions on medium heat without oil until soft. Stir continuously to avoid burning the onions. Add oil or clarified butter. Add garlic and ginger. Gently fry for 1 minute. Place marinated fish on top of mixture. Stir gently taking care not to break up the fish. Cook fish on medium heat until done. Remove pan from heat and leave covered until rice is cooked. Place fish on top of rice and garnish with fresh chopped coriander. Prepare rice as per the Bedouin Sherry Fish Stew with Rice recipe.

Bedouin Coffee

3 tbsp ground coffee
4 cups water

2 tsp cardamom powder for coffee pot or *dallah*

ROASTING METHOD:

Use a heavy frying pan that has been used for coffee roasting only because coffee will absorb the smells of food that has been cooked in the pan! Pour 2¼ cups green coffee beans into a preheated skillet. The coffee beans must be slowly and constantly stirred with a wooden spoon on medium heat to prevent burning, uneven roasting, scorching or sticking to the pan. After 10–15 minutes the coffee beans should start to turn light brown in colour. The coffee beans will start to crackle. Keep stirring! The outer shells or chaff will start to shed. Keep stirring until desired medium brown colour has been reached. Remove coffee beans from the skillet and cool while tossing or gently stirring in a large colander or pot.

GRINDING METHOD:

Once the roasted beans are cooled, use an electric coffee mill which has been used for coffee only to prevent coffee beans from absorbing smells. Grind 2¼ cups of freshly roasted coffee beans to a fine-textured grind similar to that of Turkish coffee.

BREWING THE BEDOUIN COFFEE ON STOVETOP:

Pour water in medium pot and bring to a boil. Add freshly ground coffee and simmer for 7 minutes. Remove from heat. Boil coffee. Remove coffee pot from heat after the boil and wait 5 seconds. Repeat this brewing process 2 more times.

SERVING THE BEDOUIN COFFEE FROM A DALLAH:

Dallah is the Arabic name for coffee pot, specifically designed to pour the Bedouin Coffee (also known as 'Emirati Coffee'). Remove the pot from the stove and allow the coffee grounds to settle at bottom of pot. Add cardamom into the *dallah* or coffee pot. Pour the Bedouin Coffee into *dallah* or into a coffee pot while hot. Pour the Bedouin Coffee with your left hand and hold the demi-cup in your right hand while filling it half full. It is a sign of respect to be served the half-filled demi-cup with the right hand allowing the person to drink the Bedouin Coffee in 3 sips to avoid burning the lips and tongue. Remember: Bedouin Coffee is never taken with sugar! Enjoy the wonderful fragrance of the cardamom and the simplicity of Bedouin Coffee!

This sweet, smooth comfort drink is perfumed with cardamom and bergamot from the earl grey tea, originating from India and Pakistan.

Chai Karak

SERVES 6–8

3 tbsp loose black tea, powdered
¼ cup sugar
4 cups water
1 pinch saffron threads pinch
1¾ cup condensed milk
1 tsp earl grey tea
¼ tsp cardamom (optional)

Boil water and sugar in a 2-litre pot. Remove from heat and add powdered tea, saffron, condensed milk, earl grey tea, cardamom and bring mixture to a boil. Place pot back on heat and simmer for an additional 20 minutes. Serve immediately.

Balaleet

SWEET WHEAT VERMICELLI WITH EGGS AND ONION

SERVES 8–10

INGREDIENTS FOR BALALEET:

500 g wheat vermicelli (preferably made in the United Arab Emirates)
1 medium onion, peeled and thinly sliced
8 cups water
¼ cup sugar
1 tsp saffron powder
½ cup clarified butter
1 tsp cardamom powder
4 eggs, lightly beaten
4 eggs, lightly beaten for omelette
salt to taste

Dry-roast vermicelli in a pan on medium heat, without oil or butter, until the vermicelli is light brown in colour. This may take a few minutes. Boil water in a large pot and add the vermicelli and cook for 3 minutes. Drain and transfer to a large bowl. Add sugar and carefully toss until the sugar has dissolved completely. Add saffron and cardamom powder and mix gently. Cover pot with a lid wrapped in a tea towel. This will absorb the excess liquid while the mixture is kept warm. Heat butter in a pan over medium heat and fry sliced onion until light amber in colour. Add salt and the 4 lightly beaten eggs. Gently stir the mixture until eggs are cooked. Gently toss the egg and onion mixture into the noodles. Cover *balaleet* mixture with a clean kitchen towel. Heat a frying pan until it becomes hot. Add oil and gently fry the lightly beaten 4 eggs until the eggs have firmed up. Gently flip the omelette to the other side and fry for another half a minute. Place the omelette on top of the *balaleet* mixture. Serve.

FATIMA AL QUBAISI

ABU DHABI

WITTY AND FAST

I interviewed my best friend Azza Al Qubaisi's mother, Fatima. What a woman: dynamic, witty, interesting and quick on the draw!!! The first thing Fatima said to me when we met was: 'Alexandra, let's go to the fish market first. Follow me in your car. *Yallah* Alexandra. ('hurry up!') We are late because I was in the Al Khattam desert harvesting *arta* for our dish today. *Yallah*!'

Off she bolted to the Abu Dhabi Mina Fish Market. From that moment on I knew that this interview would be exciting! While driving I asked myself what Fatima meant by harvesting *arta* in Al Khattam?

Three minutes later Fatima and I parked our cars and went inside the Fish Market to 'experience the Emirati dry fish or stockfish selection method'.

As she picked up a large stockfish, Fatima demonstrated how Emirati women choose their dry unsalted fish. She said: 'Emirati women know their food rituals, which encompass tactile, olfactory, gustatory and visual experience.'

She touched, smelled and tasted (by discreetly placing the finger that touched the fish on her tongue) then the stockfish was inspected visually from all sides. The tactile experience throws light on the importance of touching food in the daily activities of the Emirati women. This is one of Fatima's favourite food rituals that she enjoys teaching to all her children while she prepares her traditional Emirati dishes.

While Fatima was proudly demonstrating the experience of selecting dry salted and unsalted fish, she would test for texture and colour by squeezing the fish firmly on all sides. The fish passed her strict testing methods!

We soon drove back to her villa where Fatima's family and friends were expecting us for the interview and preparation of traditional dishes. The family welcomed me with open arms and I was introduced to Fatima's husband, Dr. Al Qubaisi, Ph.D. who proudly told me that he married his cousin Fatima who shares the same last name and tribe that originates from Liwa Oasis known for its extensive date farming.

'Let's proceed with the interview', announced Fatima, who then explained that she had been to Al Khattam desert in Al Ain that morning to harvest 1 kg of *machicha*. In the United Arab Emirates, *machicha* is used for *arta* which is one of the most important plants consumed by Emiratis, especially by the Bedus in the past.

Fatima was quick to explain that *arta* is a plant with many uses. Fatima's mother used the *arta's* smokeless wood in fires for cooking purposes while she included young shoots for rice, warm milk and salads. This astringent plant was also used as a tonic to cure stomach issues, or toning or colouring women's hair. Her mother would add the young, green, flexible shoots and stems to her favourite rice dishes and milk while she used the stalk and dry leaves to relieve toothaches. The bright little red seed pod lanterns were used to season rice. The *arta* is native to the Sahara and Negev deserts and can be found in many areas of the United Arab Emirates.

Indeed, the young shoots were very astringent and sour, but with the addition of minced onion they became a slightly bitter mixture, which, when added to rice or salad, became a tasty dish.

During the interview Fatima taught me the old and forgotten Emirati recipes and it was an exercise in quick multi-tasking: taking photographs while writing down her recipes! Fatima works, thinks, cooks, and enjoys talking at an incredible speed!

Machicha Fish with Rice

SERVES 6–8

Gather a large bunch of young *machicha* (approximately 500 g). You will find *machicha* in the desert, for example, in Al Khattam which is halfway to Al Ain in the Emirate of Abu Dhabi. Make sure to gather *arta* away from the road to ensure cleanliness. You should also have permission to harvest this wonder plant as *arta*, one of the most important plants in Bedu folklore, is under threat of local extinction in areas of intense camel grazing.

This long forgotten and authentic Emirati Bedouin recipe incorporates many steps but it is well worth the effort. This recipe is one of Fatima's favourite!

INGREDIENTS FOR SHERRY FISH:

2 kg sherry fish, cleaned and cut into 4 cm pieces (cut tail off)
3 tbsp vegetable oil
1 tsp turmeric powder
1 tsp salt
½ tsp chilli powder

INGREDIENTS FOR RICE:

1 cup basmati rice
4 cups cold water
½ tsp salt
2 green cardamom pods
¼ tsp whole black peppercorns
1½ garlic cloves, peeled

SHERRY FISH:

Heat oil in large pan. Add sherry fish, turmeric, salt and chilli powder. Fry on medium heat until the fish is lightly crisp and cooked. When cooked, cover and set aside.

RICE:

Rinse basmati until water runs clear. Soak it for 30 minutes in cold water. Drain. Bring water to a boil. Add rice and other ingredients. Bring to a boil, then simmer until rice is done (15–18 minutes). Remove rice from heat and drain completely. Cover rice and set aside.

TOMATO SAUCE:

Soak sour tamarind in 2 cups of water for 20 minutes. Heat oil in pan. Add onions, garlic, tomatoes and chilli. Fry for 3 minutes on medium heat. Add sweet paprika and keep stirring on low heat for 10 minutes or until onions are cooked. Meanwhile, sieve sour tamarind with your hands, or use wooden spoon. Pour sieved tamarind into the sauce and simmer for 10 minutes. Keep leftover tamarind (what was left behind in the sieve) for another recipe and refrigerate or freeze. Add fried sherry fish and 1 cup water. Cover and cook on medium heat for 10 minutes. Cover to keep warm and set aside.

INGREDIENTS FOR TOMATO SAUCE:

4 large onions, peeled and sliced
4 garlic cloves, peeled and crushed
2 large tomatoes, sliced
1 green chilli, sliced
1 tbsp sweet paprika powder
2 tbsp vegetable oil
¼ kg sour tamarind
3 cups water

INGREDIENTS FOR MACHICHA OR ARTA:

6–8 young machicha shoots, 20 cm long

MACHICHA OR ARTA:

Wash young shoots by hand with plenty of water so that all dirt is removed. Change water as often as necessary. Cut *machicha* (*arta*) shoots with a long and sharp knife as small as possible. Chopping them very small will ensure easier pounding in a sturdy metal / stone mortar which will make it easier to chew. Pound cleaned *arta* in a mortar and pestle until soft.

FISH RICE DISH:

Take half of the cooked rice and add pounded *arta* and half of the fish sauce. Debone half of the fish in the serving dish and add to rice mixture. Mix well. Serve on a platter. The rest of the sauce with the fish will be deboned while eating. Serve on a platter. You have now successfully cooked a traditional Bedouin *machicha* dish!

NADIA AL HAMELI
LIWA, ABU DHABI

'People say that I am one of the best *mohalla* makers in Liwa.'

I was curious to meet Nadia Al Hameli, known amongst her immediate and extended family as a great traditional cook and a talented embroidery designer. I was touched by Nadia's sweet, kind nature, an attentive wife and mother. She has dedicated her life to her husband and children's well-being.

During our initial conversation, Nadia shared that she was originally from Egypt, a historic country on the northeast corner of continental Africa. Nadia reflected back to her life on the family farm with great fondness and emotion. She felt blessed for her time spent outdoors at her parents' home and the loving relationship she shared with her mother and sisters.

When Nadia spoke of her intricate woven silver embroidery and golden threads *telli*, sewing, cooking, playing with her children and generally watching over her family she had a sense of great accomplishment which is warmly reflected by her quiet, unassuming smile. Nadia has a modest demeanour and expresses herself more through her hobbies than through her spoken word. Her eyes cast a gaze that speaks of her learned awareness and sense of self. Through her gift for preparing exceptional cuisine the wisdom of Nadia's years is further manifested.

Nadia's daughter Hamda trained through the mentorship of Azza Al Qubaisi who also originates from the Liwa oasis. Hamda was instrumental in arranging this interview. She was also my translator and expressed the same energy and enthusiasm as her mother.

Liwa is southwest of Abu Dhabi on the edge of the Empty Quarter Desert. My husband and I drove through the region which extends from the southern part of the Emirate of Abu Dhabi to the border of Saudi Arabia. When travelling from Al Ain, the Liwa Oasis, which is well-known for its date farms, extends to the border of Saudi Arabia and Oman.

Upon arriving at Nadia's double villa, one for women and the other for men, my husband, who is fluent in 'classical Arabic', was invited to stay and rest with the men. They had been eagerly waiting to exchange thoughts with him in Arabic while eating traditional Emirati welcome dishes which was followed by a plentiful lunch. None of the men seemed to have minded or noticed even, that they had been resting on traditional mattresses next to a falcon!

I was invited to stay with the women and children who had prepared fresh Arabic coffee, sweet tea and trays of assorted fresh dates and fruits. It was once again a delightful new taste experience for me.

We were comfortably seated in the *majlis* sitting area enjoying the unusual quietness of Nadia's home; no trucks and virtually no cars passed by. Only large trees and empty, sandy roads. What a pleasure for us coming from the city!

Nadia was wearing an abaya, a long black robe, a *hijab*, a head and neck scarf, and a golden *burqa*, a facial mask covering the mouth and nose but highlighting the eyes, which is attached under the *hijab*. She has been wearing a *burqa* ever since she was a young girl. The *burqa*, very much a Gulf area garment, is still worn today but mostly by older Emirati women.

Nadia was very excited to be interviewed and enthusiastically explained: 'Liwa is known for its annual 'Date Festival' and we are proud to showcase approximately forty-five different types of Emirati dates. This is our annual heritage event where virtually every family in Liwa actively engages in the festival in one way or another. My family, the 'Al Hameli's, has been in Liwa for a very long time and we are well known here.'

The Al Hameli family was amongst other Emirati families of the Liwa Oasis who cultivated date palm trees and kept chickens, camels and goats in order to feed their large family. Even today, many families still maintain a similar way of life integrated with modern lifestyles. We used to live in houses made out of palm fronds and we protected ourselves from the moving sand by constructing fences out of palm fronds as well.

I asked Nadia about her *telli* weaving talents. She proudly told me: 'I learned to be a *telli* weaver from my mother-in-law shortly after I arrived from my wedding in my native Egypt. I had to be very confident to be able to accomplish the art of *telli* weaving. I will show you how I weave on my *telli* which I work on as often as I can. It is one of my favourite hobbies! Women enjoy my woven embroideries which are applied to the sleeves and bodice of traditional Emirati dress.

Nadia eagerly demonstrated her *telli* skills, and explained that the woven pieces are in fact a type of embroidery where numerous coloured threads are twisted one after another. She continued to explain the workings of her twenty-five-year old *telli* stand: 'In the middle I have a *khousa* which is a silver coloured lace panel adjusted on a piece of metal which we call *kajuja*, and on top you will be able to see a metal bracket. This is to stabilize the threads while I am twisting the colours to create popular traditional Emirati designs such as *bafutlutan*, *badla*, *bawadil* and many more. Nadia's eyes are kind, alert and they sparkled as she patiently awaited my next question.

As lunch was approaching she said: 'We will eat *semach mashway*, a grilled fish on a large mountain of rice with some cooked vegetables. My husband caught ample fish for all twenty of us and my kitchen helpers grilled the fish and cooked the rice.'

All the women assisted in carrying the dishes from the kitchen located outside the house which were then placed on a plastic tablecloth on the floor. A very large metal platter heaped with rice and enough grilled fish to feed us several times over was placed in the center of the tablecloth. It was surrounded by small plates of salad, yoghurt, homemade pickles, hot sauces and more fish on separate plates!

Nadia is intuitive and artful at enhancing her dishes with spices that exude exquisite fragrances and flavours, a culinary delight to all the senses. *Semach mashway* was truly a traditional Emirati delicacy!

As Nadia finished lunch first, she announced: 'After lunch *mohalla*, a bread sweetened with only dates!'

Shortly before my husband and I were ready to drive back to Abu Dhabi, Nadia gave us date and fruit baskets made from sun-dried palm fronds. I was touched by her gifts which I now use to decorate my rooms in Berlin for my Emirati themed workshops. Nadia's recipe is simply exquisite and must be tried!

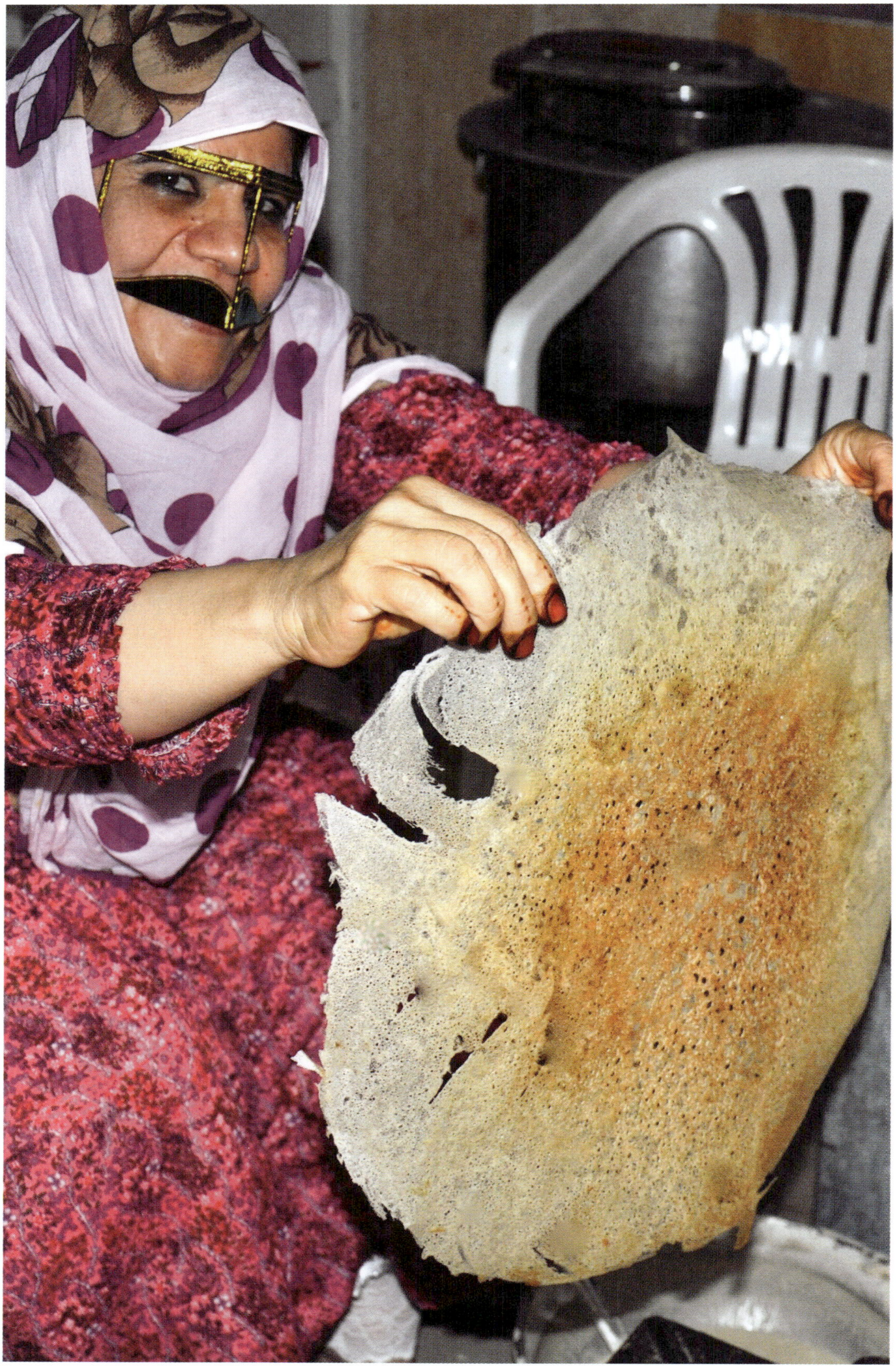

Mohalla

PAPER THIN DATE CREPE-LIKE BREAD

SERVES 6–8

Mohalla is an unleavened, paper-thin traditional bread that Emirates eat for breakfast, lunch and dinner. It's also very popular during Ramadan. The date crepe-like bread is made on a large circular iron dish called a *tabi* which is used to make *rgaag*. The liquid batter is placed on the tabi over direct heat. The edges are carefully scraped using a spatula then it's folded and served hot.

3 cups flour
1 ½ cups soft dates, pitted
1 tsp salt
2–3 cups water
ghee (clarified butter) for the *tabi*
1 bowl water for your hands
1 *tabi* (available online or at some ethnic stores)

Soak dates for 45 minutes in 2 cups of hot water. The length of the soak will depend on the softness of the dates. Hand squeeze soaked dates in the same water until they are pureed. Mix flour and salt in a medium-sized bowl, then slowly add ½ of the pureed date liquid. Mix all ingredients with your hands. Add more date water if needed and with one hand knead while beating batter against the bowl, lifting it and repeating. This method of beating against the bowl is to remove lumps.

Repeat this process until the batter is smooth and has the consistency of heavy whipping cream. The batter should have a thickness that allows it to be easily spread around the tabi. Add more water if needed. Should you have leftover date water, do not discard; store it in the refrigerator. The liquid is good for smoothies, or to simply enjoy as a healthy Bedouin date cooling drink. Cover batter with a kitchen towel and leave to rest for 30 minutes in a warm area.

Place the *tabi* on a direct flame and spread a little ghee on it with a paper towel; this is to prevent the batter from sticking to it. Once the *tabi* is hot, take a ladle (about ¾ cup–1 cup) of batter and pour it on the outer edge of the *tabi*. Spread the batter in circular motions until you have filled the entire surface of the *tabi*. Holes can be quickly filled by dabbing a bit of batter on them. Use a carpenter's metal spatula to lift the bread once the edges are light brown and crisp. A steady hand will ensure that the *mohalla* bread doesn't break.

Don't be discouraged; it takes time and practice to master the making of *mohalla* bread! *Mohalla* should be eaten hot, drizzled with honey, molasses or date syrup. Eggs, ghee or cheese can be added as well.

MARIAM AND SALIMA AL YAMMAHI
THE FUJAIRAH MOUNTAINS

TWO BEAUTIFUL, OPEN-HEARTED WOMEN WHO LIVE WITH THEIR HUSBAND IN THE FUJAIRAH MOUNTAINS

My friend Azza Al Qubaisi and her family drove me to the Fujairah Hajar mountains facing the small village of Tawaeen, located approximately 30 km from the city of Fujairah. This is where Mariam, Salima and their common husband Mohammed's home was nestled amid a large number of palm trees. The family resided there while their new villa was being constructed in the village of Tawaeen.

Mohammed, a tall, calm, religious and humble man welcomed us with open arms, proud to present his two beautiful wives, cousins Mariam and Salima. Salima, an Economics student in Fujairah, and the younger of the two cousins, was assisting me with the translation.

Mariam and Salima served a farm style *fualah*. The dishes were placed on the floor on a sarrut or date palm tree leaves mat which both women enjoy creating. Mariam is teaching Salima the art of plaiting palm leaves into baskets, mats, handbags and miniature national flags for schools and has always included their traditional family designs recognized as the 'Al Yammahi' family designs. The *fualah* was composed of water, juices, *harees* and Emirati cheese known as *chammi* served with clarified butter and dates. Heavenly!

Bread, olives, chickpeas, peeled mangoes and a fruit basket were also part of the *fualah*. These elaborate farm style dishes were served in the main *majlis* (a place of sitting) designed for women. The men had the same dishes but they were served outside under the turquoise blue sky.

While eating the *fualah*, women shared stories about their local traditional cuisine and the latest news about their respective families. I was profoundly honoured by all that they shared in my presence.

After our *fualah*, Mohammed sectioned the lamb slaughtered that morning and hooked it on wire. The marinated pieces of meat were lowered and hung inside a preheated earth cooking pit. The meat was covered with jute bags, wood and a sheet of metal topped with rocks to trap the heat but also to prevent animals from scrounging the meat. Mohammed maintained that cooking in an earth oven is a very effective method of baking any type of meat. He was proud to tell us that many of his friends still use the earth oven, often referred to as a *tandoor*, for all their large functions.

It was evident that Mariam enjoyed cooking outdoors. Her husband designed a metal tandoor oven situated close to their villa kitchen. The oven was fired with wood gathered from the mountains. Mohammed also constructed a support for the *tabi*, a large, circular, iron plate placed over the fire on which *rgaag* was cooked. Mariam's pots and pans were hung on conveniently located trees, making their outdoor cooking a pleasant experience.

Mariam and Salima proudly prepared *al yammahi*, a cinnamon, cardamom and saffron flavoured rice dish cooked outdoors on a gas fire. The pungent aroma of the spices wafted everywhere as 70 cm circular trays were heaped with rice. The lamb was placed on top and decorated with fresh herbs. Men and women were served in their separate seating areas. Before they started eating, the guests clearly but discreetly uttered the word *Bismillah* which means 'In the Name of Allah' as a thank you for the food they were about to receive. My visit turned out to be an astounding flavour experience with women who enjoy cooking.

Young Lamb in an Oven Pit

SERVES 10–12

5–7 kg young lamb, cut into hand-sized pieces
3 tbsp salt
3 tbsp turmeric powder
⅓ cup *bzar* (see page 15)
1 bunch radish tails or *rowaid*
coriander and parsley to garnish

Mix salt, turmeric and *bzar* and spread on each piece of meat. Marinate in the refrigerator for 1 hour. Hook meat on wires and hang in oven pit or grill. Cover with wet jute bags, wood and a sheet of metal topped with rocks to trap the heat. After 2 hours check meat to see if it is juicy and tears easily. If the meat is still tough leave for another 1–2 hours. Doneness will depend on the size of the meat. Remove all covers, lift the meat and transfer to a large recipient. If you used wires or hooks to hold the meat in place, make sure to remove them. Serve in a circle on top of rice laid out in a large, round tray. Garnish with radish tails or *rowaid*, coriander and parsley.

Circular trays are used so that every guest is treated equally and has equal access to the rice and lamb from their seating position. This is very much part of the Emirati social food ritual.

Al Yammahi Rice Dish

SERVES 12–16

6 kg basmati rice
¼ cup oil
6 onions, thinly sliced
2 bell peppers, thinly sliced and chopped
1 tsp saffron threads
1 stick cassia (4 inches)
5 whole cardamom pods
3 tbsp *bzar* (see page 15)
1 tsp whole coriander seeds
1 tsp whole cumin seeds
1 cup fresh parsley
1 cup fresh coriander

Soak rice in salted water for 30 minutes before lamb is finished cooking! Add ¼ cup hot water to saffron and soak for 15 minutes or until ready to be sprinkled on cooked rice. Drain rice, transfer to a pot, cover with water and add salt. Bring to a boil, then simmer until rice is half cooked. Drain and set aside, covered. Take the extra large pot, heat oil and fry onions together with the spices until onions have reached a light caramel colour. Add enough water to cover the spices. Add the drained rice, gently mix and cook until rice is done. This may take 10–15 minutes. Serve the rice on a large platter. Sprinkle the prepared saffron and top with lamb (see Mohammed's I recipe in this chapter). Garnish with coriander and parsley.

Al Yammahi Bzar

This spice mixture is Mariam Al Yammahi's specialty. She uses it in her traditional recipes and sells it commercially. Mariam experimented for a long time until she reached the perfect balance of spices. In Fujairah, this mixture is known as 'Al Yammahi *bzar* spices'. Mariam says that her *bzar* spice mixture is appreciated by Emirati women who do not have time to create their own *bzar* spices but still want the authentic Emirati mixture for their day to day recipes. As a result, Mariam prepares her signature *bzar* spice mixture on a daily basis for her clients.

3 tsp Fujairah mountains wild mushrooms, dried
½ kg turmeric powder
¼ kg whole black peppercorns
1 kg coriander seeds
250 g whole star of anise
1 kg fennel seeds (also known as sweet cumin)
½ kg whole chilli peppers, dried
250 g cassia sticks (or cinnamon sticks), broken
250 g black *loumi* powder (dried lime-available in ethnic stores or home ground)
¼ kg cloves
2 nutmegs, broken into pieces
1 kg cumin seeds
3 whole black *loumi*, cracked
½ kg small round chilli peppers

Lightly dry-roast all spices (except turmeric and *loumi* powder) over very low heat, stirring constantly until spices give off a delicious fragrance and turn golden in colour. Remove from heat and add turmeric and *loumi* powder. Cool. Grind in a mortar and pestle or in an electric grinder. Store the ground spices in an airtight container away from light. This *bzar* spice can be stored up to one year.

Harees

WHEAT PORRIDGE WITH LAMB MEAT

SERVES 16–20

Mariam looked at me with her beautiful dark eyes and in her soft-spoken voice said: 'Alexandra, remember to write in your book that *harees* is our local, traditional and most pleasing dish served during Ramadan and wedding. However, today many of us eat *harees* during the week. It's tasty and heart-warming and is eaten by all social classes in our culture.'

4 kg whole wheat grain
3 kg lamb, cut into pieces including bones
½ cup salt
5 tbsp ghee

Wash meat and cook on medium heat in large pot with a 1:1 ratio of water to meat until cooked. This may take a few hours. Ladle off froth while meat is cooking. Rinse wheat and add to the pot with meat. Add salt and cook until the meat is completely dissolved and integrated with the wheat. This may take 3–6 hours depending on whether cooked directly on fire or on stove. Add water if needed. Transfer into a clay or metal pot and top with a 2 cm layer of water. Do not mix! This is to keep the *harees* moist while it is cooking in the tandoor. Place the pot into a prepared oven pit or tandoor, cover with lid and a heavy piece of metal to trap the heat. Leave to cook all night on low smouldering wood. In the morning, remove pot from oven pit or tandoor and remove meat from the bones. Use a large wooden spoon to stir and pound or take a very large hand-held food mixer (which looks like a large cement mixer which may extend to four feet in length) and mix until the mixture is pureed. Sprinkle ghee or homemade *dehn kheneen* (clarified butter) on each serving. Serve hot.

KHAWLA AL ZAABI
ABU DHABI

'Parental warmth, love, affection, and traditional values fused with modern values are children's most important asset to becoming successful adults.'

I met Khawla Al Zaabi through her daughter Nasra whom I met at the Qasr Al Hosn annual festival in Abu Dhabi. We were finally able to arrange a time where I could observe her mother cooking traditional Emirati dishes.

Upon entering their large villa in Al Rahba outside the island of Abu Dhabi, I was welcomed by Nasra and her seven younger siblings. They had prepared a welcome *fualah* with drinks and trays of chocolates, biscuits, dates, dips, fruits and candies.

Khawla Al Zaabi joined us in the women's sitting room or *majlis* and seemed honoured to be part of my Emirati cookbook. She is a tall, elegant woman, very much in touch with her femininity. She has a formal education but has learned much more through her life experiences. She is confident and witty with an endearing sense of humour. The day of the interview she was dressed in a traditional floral-patterned Emirati dress. Khawla was masterful at conveying her traditional Emirati recipes. She also took time to share her concerns at being a good educator for her children. She confided: 'My husband and I devote our time to being strong role models for our children's educational achievements, as well as their social skills. We find it very important to incorporate our traditional Emirati social and food culture into our modern lifestyle for their sake.'

Khawla explained that the bond between herself and Nasra is very strong. Her daughter is an active team player when caring for her siblings.

'It is important that all my children teach and assist each other even for basic life skills such as tying shoes, getting dressed, put their backpacks away, fold their clothes, help clean up toys, throw away their own trash after meals and snacks, serving food and cleaning up after their younger siblings. I decided not to have housemaids for my children because this would create a dependency and prevent my children from becoming self-reliant. However, we do have a cook, farmer and housemaids for household chores but not for taking care of my children. Raising our own children gives us the opportunity to show them the value of our Emirati social and food culture. Our country is privileged and wealthy and I would like my children to convey this privileged position which includes traditional values with modern standards to the next generation.'

Coming back to the cookbook Khawla emphasized: 'I have chosen a variety of traditional dishes which are usually served with dates known as *seh* and homemade pickles.' 'We never forget to place one or two dishes of green leaves such as *rowaid* which are white radish with green leaves considered to be a delicacy, and the small, narrow and bitter tasting leaves of our well known *ghaf* tree.' It is the national tree of the United Arab Emirates. Through the Give a *ghaf* campaign, citizens are urged to plant a *ghaf* tree in their gardens to combat desertification and to preserve their country's heritage. This shows you the importance of this 'magical' tree. Most homes are expected to plant *ghaf*, *sidra*, palm, lemon and mango trees in their yards.

During the photo shoot I was shown Khawla's vegetable garden and her collection of homemade traditional pickles. We then had lunch and later on dinner. It was such a pleasure to be welcomed as if I was part of the family. This is indeed a deeply ingrained welcoming ritual amongst Emiratis who are masters at entertaining and welcoming their guests.

Bedouin Wild Ghaf Salad

SERVES 6–8

Wild *ghaf* is the national tree of the United Arab Emirates, and can be found throughout the country. An evergreen, the *ghaf* tree is considered the sturdiest plant growing in the desert, and a sign that there is a deep water table. For this reason, the *ghaf* tree does not compete with other crops for water. It is illegal to cut down a *ghaf* due to urbanization.

To ensure the tree's continuity, ask for permission from your friends who grow their own *ghaf* tree in their back yard when removing a few twigs with the leafy parts for your salad. Leaves are slightly bitter in taste and abrasive on the tongue. Hence it is vital that they be very finely chopped, adding its unique flavour to meat, poultry and rice dishes.

2 cups wild ghaf leaves, removed from the stalk, chopped
2 tbsp lime juice
1 dash pepper
1 pinch salt

Wash *ghaf* leaves thoroughly until water runs clean. Hold the knife against your knuckles and cut the *ghaf* leaves until finely chopped. Transfer to a serving bowl. Add lime juice, pepper and salt and mix well. Marinate for 1 hour during which time the abrasiveness will be reduced.

Enjoy the exploration of taste and allow your taste buds to experience this unique Bedouin wild *ghaf* salad along with Emirati meat, poultry and rice dishes. *Ghaf* is definitely a salad not to be missed when eating Emirati traditional dishes. I admit that I love the Bedouin wild *ghaf* salad!

Whole Roasted Fish

STUFFED WITH EMIRATI *KHAL* AND EXOTIC SPICES

SERVES 4–6

Mariam looked at me with her beautiful dark eyes and in her soft-spoken voice said: 'Alexandra, remember to write in your book that *harees* is our local, traditional and most pleasing dish served during Ramadan and wedding. However, today many of us eat *harees* during the week. It's tasty and heart-warming and is eaten by all social classes in our culture.'

2–3 kg fish of your choice
2 green chilli peppers, chopped, seeds removed
1 cup *khal* (see page 89)
2 tbsp *bzar* (see page 15)
1 tsp turmeric powder
1 tsp salt (or to taste)
1 tsp cumin powder
1 tsp coriander powder
1 large onion, peeled and thinly sliced
4 garlic cloves, peeled and chopped
1 cup fresh coriander, chopped, to garnish
8 lime wedges

Preheat oven to 170°C. Line roasting pan with baking paper. Clean, gut, scale fish. Cut tail off. Place fish diagonally on prepared roasting pan. Make 3 diagonal incisions on both sides of the fish, cover and set aside. Mix chopped chillies, *khal*, *bzar*, turmeric, salt, cumin and coriander. Divide spice mixture into 2 bowls: 1st Bowl: Rub whole fish with spices. 2nd Bowl: Add sliced onion and chopped garlic and stuff the belly cavity of the fish. Roast fish in preheated oven.

Fish is done when juices run clear from slashes in the flesh. Gently pull on the fin. If the fin comes away easily the fish is cooked. Transfer baked fish on a large serving platter and garnish with chopped fresh coriander and lime wedges.

A combination of a spicy tomato sauce with maleh (preserved fish), served with rice. The maleh recipe involves many steps. It is well worth the effort because it is an exquisite authentic Emirati Bedouin recipe.

Saloona with Maleh

SPICY TOMATO SAUCE WITH PRESERVED FISH

INGREDIENTS FOR PRESERVING MALEH (FOR SALTING FISH):

1 medium-large sized mackerel (*chanad* in Arabic)
4 lemon wedges
10 fresh ginger slices
1 tbsp cumin, ground
1 tbsp pepper, ground
5 red chilli peppers
10 garlic cloves, peeled
5 kg large, rough crystal salt (also known as kosher salt)
20 cups water
1 clean glass container or plastic bucket which should be a little larger than the fish. The fish will eventually drop down to the bottom of the container. Either option will require a lid.

INGREDIENTS FOR SALOONA (SPICY TOMATO SAUCE):

250 g *maleh* (preserved fish), washed, skinned, deboned, patted dry and hand shredded
2 tbsp *dehn kheneen* (clarified butter)
2 large onions, peeled and thinly sliced
4 garlic cloves, peeled and chopped
2 large tomatoes, chopped
2 green chilli peppers, sliced in half, seeded
3 cups water
2 tsp *loumi* powder
1 tbsp *bzar* (see page 15)
1 tbsp turmeric powder
1 tsp salt (or to taste)
3 *loumi*, cut in half
½ cup fresh coriander, chopped, to garnish
4 lime wedges

PRESERVING MALEH (FOR SALTING FISH):

Place mackerel in sink, wash, gut, scale and discard the head (or freeze it for when you want to make fish soup). Pour water in container and dissolve kosher salt by continuously stirring. This process may take 5–10 minutes. Place mackerel in container. Add lemon wedges, ginger slices, cumin, pepper, chilli peppers and garlic cloves. Cover and label it. Leave fish to salt from 6 months to 2 years in a dry, dark and cold room. Once the fish has marinated for at least 6 months and you wish to serve it, rinse, skin, debone and pat dry with kitchen paper. It has now become *maleh*, you can start all the other recipes which follow: Saloona with *maleh*, *maleh* dressing, Emirati *khal* and rice dish.

SALOONA (SPICY TOMATO SAUCE):

Heat butter in large, heavy saucepan over medium heat. Add onion, garlic and crushed green chilli peppers. Stir and cook until onion is translucent. Add remaining ingredients, stir occasionally and simmer for about 30 minutes or until sauce thickens.

INGREDIENTS FOR RICE:

2 cups basmati rice
8 cups cold water
2 tbsp *dehn kheneen* (clarified butter)
1 tsp salt
3 green cardamom pods
½ tsp whole black peppercorns

INGREDIENTS FOR EMIRATI KHAL (LIME JUICE AND SALT MIXTURE):

½ cup large, rough crystal salt (also known as kosher salt)
1½ cups lime juice, freshly pressed
1 sealable sterilized glass bottle

INGREDIENTS FOR MALEH DRESSING (FOR SALADS):

2 onions, peeled and thinly sliced
5 chilli peppers, chopped
1 cup water
½ cup *khal*

INGREDIENTS FOR GARNISH:

½ cup fresh coriander, chopped
½ cup fresh coriander
4 lemon wedges

RICE:

Rinse basmati rice until water runs clear. Soak for 30 minutes in cold water. Drain rice and put in large pot along with spices. Bring to a boil, add *dehn kheneen* and simmer until rice is cooked. Drain rice completely.

KHAL:

Mix lime juice and kosher salt in a glass bottle that can be sealed. Shake *khal* mixture until completely dissolved. Seal and store *khal* mixture up to 1 year in a cold and dark room. The aging process of the *khal* mixture improves the quality and the taste will become stronger. You can start using *khal* mixture after 1 month.

MALEH DRESSING

Mix all ingredients and pour on *maleh*.

Khawla Al Zaabi proudly explained: 'Khal is also known as a very old Emirati Bedouin mixture used to alleviate symptoms such as nausea and stomach ailments.'

HOW TO SERVE MALEH SALAD

Slice or tear preserved *maleh* (preserved fish) into pieces. Place on a platter and pour all of the dressing on it.Decorate with lemon wedges, chopped and whole coriander. Serve *maleh* with rice and *saloona* sauce. Guests spoon *saloona* on the rice and eat with *maleh*.

MARIAM HAMMAT
AJMAN

A MOTHER OF NINE CHILDREN MAINTAINING A BALANCE BETWEEN TRADITIONAL BEDOUIN CULTURE AND MODERN LIFE.

I had finished interviews for my cookbook in Fujairah and wanted to take the bus from Fujairah to Ajman via Dubai. However, the bus was unavailable for reasons that escaped me. Azza Al Qubaisi's husband Moaid was able to find me a taxi in the early hours of the morning. I was relieved to know that I would be able to make it to Ajman to interview Mariam Hammat.

My taxi driver assured me that he would be able to bring me to the address I had given him. But shortly after arriving in Ajman he looked at me and said: 'Madam, where do you want to go?' 'Madam, my car only knows Ajman Mall.' 'Madam, go out now!'

At this moment I realized that flexibility was called for. Instead of becoming upset I agreed to being dropped off at the Ajman Mall and called Mariam who went out of her way to pick me up. Mariam revealed that she would be cooking for me at her mother's villa. She also mentioned that her family was being relocated from her original fifty-year old home to a beautiful new and very large villa in an urban area located in the centre of Ajman. One of the memorable landscapes of Ajman is its beautiful expanse of powder-like white sand which spans almost twenty miles, flanking the shores of the Persian Gulf Coast.

'I am very happy with our new villa,' Mariam told me. 'We have Bedouin welcoming areas throughout the villa which in Arabic are called *majlis*. One is for women and the other is for men and they are decorated with carpets and colourful floor cushions.'

Mariam went on to explain that the tribal etiquette amongst the Bedouins is to ensure that the tradition of 'being respectful to oneself as well as to others' is transferred to the next generations. 'We are very proud of our culture and we will make sure that it is well-integrated in our modern way of living. Our lives have changed dramatically, no doubt for the better. However, we maintain our Bedouin traditions in order to make sure that our heritage will never be lost or forgotten.'

Mariam went on to say that she is proud to be from Bedouin background and would like to help me record one of her favourite traditional Bedouin dishes for my cookbook. Her eyes lit up when she mentioned that she had nine children and casually mentioned that they were all hers, of which three graduated from college, the other four married with children of their own, and that the others were still attending primary school.

A few days prior to my arrival Mariam had won the amateur cooking prize: a twenty-four carat gold coin in a round golden box. The culinary event was held at the International Competition of the 2014 Dubai World Hospitality Championship at which the United Arab Emirates professional team won first place.

Mariam's passion for cooking is undeniable. I was given a large plate filled to the rim with *aseeda*, a delicious sweet dish composed of toasted wheat and pureed carrots, a generous measure of saffron and drizzled with clarified butter.

'Enjoy! This is Bedouin hospitality. My *aseeda* is the best and most memorable slow-cooked dish that you have ever tasted!' Mariam exclaimed proudly. Indeed, Mariam was right. Her *aseeda* is simply the best!

Aseeda is a unique taste experience well worth the time and effort needed to recreate Mariam Hammat's version. Emiratis love aseeda and eat it any time of the day and for all occasions.

Aseeda with Carrots

SWEET CARROT PUDDING

SERVES 6–8

Aseeda has a pudding-like consistency similar to soft play dough. It's made of toasted wheat, clarified butter and saffron. Mariam Hammat explained that *aseeda* can be eaten sweet or savoury and can be cooked with dates, different types of flours, pumpkin, sweet potatoes or carrots. *Aseeda* with carrots is one of Mariam's favourite sweet dishes.

4 large carrots
6 cups water
⅔ cup sugar
3 cups whole wheat flour
⅓ cup dhen kheneen (Emirati clarified butter)
1 ½ tsp cardamom powder
2 tsp saffron threads
4 tbsp dhen kheneen

Wash, peel and cut carrots into thick slices. Bring medium sized pot of water to a boil, add carrots making sure they are covered with water. Cover pot and cook carrots over medium heat until soft. Drain and transfer carrots to a stand mixer. Add 2 cups water to the carrots and puree. Cover and set aside. Put the flour in a heavy skillet or large pot and place over medium heat. Stir the flour constantly while the flour is toasting to prevent burning! For a medium toast similar to light caramel colour, it will take 5–7 minutes. Remove from heat, cool, sieve, cover and set aside on medium heat. Caramelizing sugar: place sugar in a deep saucepan on medium heat. Gently stir sugar with a wooden spoon and move the liquefied sugar from the edges to the center until it has melted. This is to prevent sugar from burning. Stir until sugar has turned amber or light brown in colour. This may take up to 10 minutes. Remove saucepan from heat and place on wooden board. Carefully pour 4 cups of water in caramelized sugar. It will sputter and bubble up vigorously! Put saucepan back to heat and stir. Add pureed carrots, saffron, cardamom and stir over medium-low heat. Add ⅓ cup of *dhen kheneen*, cook and stir for approximately 7 minutes. Slowly add toasted flour to carrot mixture and turn heat off. Stir for 3–4 minutes until mixture has thickened, is lump free and texture has become smooth, similar to soft play dough. Spoon half the mixture on a deep serving platter, shaping by hand and leveling the top with a spatula. Pour 2 tbsp of *dhen kheneen* over *aseeda* and swirl with the back of a spoon until glossy. Do not mix! Finish by spooning the second half of the mixture on top of the first layer, shaping by hand and leveling with a spatula. Pour 2 tbsp of *dhen kheneen* over *aseeda* and swirl with the back of a spoon until glossy. Do not mix. Best served warm.

MONA AL ZAABI
DUBAI

'COOKING TRADITIONAL EMIRATI DISHES IS MY PASSION, AND IT KEEPS MY HUSBAND HAPPY!'

What a fascinating family! Khawla Al Zaabi, whom I had interviewed just a few hours before, decided spontaneously to take Nasra and I, a few of her younger children, her sister Maryam, her five children and the housekeeper to visit Mona, another sister who resides in Dubai. Upon arrival it seemed like a nev er ending number of passengers were descending from the car.

Visiting each other is a weekly routine, one that has been going on for years. As soon as we arrived, we disappeared amongst the vast number of wings in the villa. I was introduced to the family and guests who were joyously chatting away in the ladies sitting room, known as the ladies' *majlis* as well as in the other receiving areas and the large kitchens.

Mona Al Zaabi was in the kitchen cooking as well as delegating her team of kitchen assistants barely twenty-four hours after she had undergone surgery. What a show! For a short moment, I forgot why I had been invited. My fascination at the abundance of food being prepared and the large number of family members and guests fully distracted me.

I took my camera and started the photo shoot, taking notes for this interview, while Mona was also attending to her family members and guests who were invited to help in the preparations for one of Mona's daughter's upcoming marriage. They were also dispersed in the various other kitchens cooking, baking and exchanging family stories. I realized I had to work fast!

Mona is a born cook and passionate manager. I was able to photograph the two dishes for my cookbook while she was moving from one kitchen to the next, explaining her recipes, while filling me in on her background. I was even able to taste every dish including those for the upcoming wedding!

This interview was one of the fastest I have ever experienced and a true learning experience! There is no better way to learn than from traditional, passionate cooks like Mona Al Zaabi. I hovered over her while shooting the dishes, and she would say: 'Alexandra, my passion for cooking was transmitted to me and to all the women in my family through the generations. The question is who amongst the women experiences true enthusiasm for cooking our Emirati traditional dishes?

My priority is to keep my husband happy so I cook him his favourite dishes! It is in our culture to express our acknowledgment of family, friends and guests through personal versions of traditional Emirati dishes. Food is God's most precious gift and that is why I enjoy creating traditional as well as modern dishes. It is our way of being together and enjoying each other's company.

In our Emirati culture, food has a deeply rooted connection to God and it is interwoven with rituals that teach us to appreciate and experience what we are eating through touch, smell, taste and presentation. Emirati women and men who enjoy cooking make sure that their dishes always taste better than that of other cooks. Presentation must be outstanding in order for the cook to be remembered!'

Khawla Al Zaabi entered the kitchen when I had just finished interviewing Mona. She announced that we were all driving to her brother's home, Obaid Saif Al Zaabi, who lived just twenty minutes away and where we would enjoy a traditional Emirati buffet dinner catered by one of his friends.

I realized that I had to stop eating to make room for a large traditional Emirati buffet dinner. I had already been fed generous helpings of Mona's creations!

We all sat on cushions under a starlit sky, surrounded by numerous date palm trees. I stopped counting the number of family members, friends and guests. The numbers kept increasing by the hour and I assume that we must have reached close to seventy people sharing this marvellous dining experience! The Al Zaabi family truly impressed me. They are a warm and kind-hearted family and they know how to maintain their traditional Emirati team spirit!

Chbaab

SERVES 6–8

'I have become the best *chbaab* maker amongst my family. My mother explained the importance of not only becoming a great cook, but to set the accent on serving and presenting my creations with love. This always results in the dishes becoming more appealing than that of any other cook! I still enjoy this well-kept secret'

3 cups water
1 cup whole wheat flour
1 cup white flour
½ cup milk
1 large egg
1 tbsp instant dry yeast
½ tsp saffron threads
1 pinch cardamom powder
1 pinch turmeric powder
4 tbsp dried coconut, shredded
Vegetable oil for a non-stick pan
2 tsp date syrup for each chbaab (or more if desired)
2 tbsp thick laban (similar to cream cheese) for each chbaab

Combine flours, yeast, saffron, cardamom, turmeric and coconut in mixer and stir on low speed until well combined. Add egg, milk and slowly add water and mix until you have a batter that has the consistency of liquid cream. Cover bowl with a clean kitchen tea towel and place *chbaab* mixture into the oven (with the light on) and leave for 30 minutes. Heat a nonstick pan on medium and brush with ½ teaspoon of oil for each *chbaab*. Pour ⅓ cup of batter for each *chbaab*. Cook until bubbles form and the edges become slightly dry. Turn *chbaab* and cook until light golden brown on underside. Drizzle with date syrup and dip each *chbaab* and dip in *laban*.

Mona's *chbaab* is indeed something to die for! It doesn't get better than this. Mona kept her promise: you will feel a flavour explosion of saffron, cardamom and toasted coconut in your mouth as you bite into these *chaabs*.

Find yourself in a traditional Emirati tent and you cannot resist the smell of baking khameer while sipping Emirati coffee infused with cardamom. You will melt with pleasure as soon as you have filled one or more khameer with your favourite fillings. Enjoy!

Bedouin Khameer

ROUND YEAST FLATBREAD

SERVES 8–10

INGREDIENTS FOR BREAD:

2½ cups water
1 cup whole wheat flour
1 cup white flour
½ cup yoghurt
1 tbsp instant dry yeast
½ tsp saffron threads
1 pinch cardamom powder
1 pinch turmeric powder
3 large eggs, for egg wash
khameer pot with a heating element (made in Iran and available at selected Iranian and Indian stores)

INGREDIENTS FOR FILLINGS:

1 small bowl date syrup or thick chammi (similar to cream cheese), honey, sugar, cream cheese, molasses, dhen kheneen

Combine flours, yeast, saffron, cardamom, turmeric in bowl and mix on low speed. Add yoghurt and slowly add water. Continue pouring and mixing until the batter has a thick consistency. Cover bowl with a clean tea towel and place khameer mixture into the oven (with oven light on) and leave to rise until double in size. Punch dough and knead until smooth. Roll out the dough on floured surface using a rolling pin. To obtain circular shaped khameer, cut dough with a medium sized cup or use an extra-large round cookie cutter or… take a small handful of dough and pat each into a circular shape. You may need to use a few drops of water on your hands if they become sticky. If the cup or extra-large cookie cutter is sticking, dip into flour and continue cutting until all the dough is used up.

USING KHAMEER POT:

Place 1 round of dough on top of the medium heated and ungreased *khameer*. Bake until bubbles appear, brush on egg wash and sprinkle with sesame seeds (optional). When the bread rises and the underside turns light brown, remove it from the top of the pan, and carefully place it inside the pot under the grill until the top is light brown. Be careful not to burn the *khameer*. Check often!Continue baking dough in the same manner. Place baked *khameer* on a large serving platter surrounded by the fillings. Gently cut or open the warm *khameer* and fill it with any or a combination of the fillings.

HANAN RASHID HAMDAN AL SHOOKRI
ABU DHABI

'MY PASSION IS TO TEACH MY CHILDREN TO COOK AND LOOK AFTER THEMSELVES.'

'In an era where motherhood is as important as pursuing a career, I decided to become a part time stay-at-home mother for my five children, and I work at the Cleveland Hospital as a Health Unit Coordinator. This is my most precious gift to my children while they are developing into young adults' says Hanan Rashid Hamdan. Hanan graduated from Health Information Management at the Higher School of Technology in Abu Dhabi.

Hanan is a young, loving and kind-hearted mother who was born in Abu Dhabi's Corniche Hospital. Hanan's parents originated from Al Ain, about two hours from the island of Abu Dhabi. Her husband Hamdan Al Shekaili works as an Engineer.

Both parents have been gifted land by the Sheikh Zayed bin Sultan Al Nahyan Foundation, Abu Dhabi, in order to encourage the construction of their home and raise their children and extended family in a healthy and comfortable environment. Hamdan, together with his brother, is having a large villa constructed in Al Foah, a suburb at the north end of the historic garden city of Al Ain. Eventually the villas will be the home of both brothers and their respective families.

'Emiratis enjoy and prefer to be amongst their families for all social gatherings. A strong sense of family is a long-standing tradition amongst our Emirati culture. We will have two large *majlis*, which are sitting rooms with low-sitting sofas spread along the walls of the living room. This arrangement is to seat our large families in our new villa. In our culture we segregate our gathering and have one *majlis* for women and another for men,' Hanan proclaimed. Women enjoy networking and chatting amongst themselves and this goes for the men as well.

One of Hanan's passions is cooking and she is full of adventure and surprises when she teaches traditional Emirati dishes to her children. She insists on imparting the art of respect in preparing dishes through story-telling and reading. Hanan always has time to assist her children with their school homework. She has decided to have Fares, one of her sons, attend the German International School (GISA) in Abu Dhabi. 'Fares will be the only child from my family to be able to speak three languages: Arabic, English and German. This may eventually lead him to conduct business between the United Arab Emirates and Germany,' gushed Hanan proudly.

'I wanted to experience a different culture, language and school life when I was younger, in addition to my regular Emirati schooling. A new language is one of the main reasons why I chose an international school for my son Fares. I have always wanted to experience a new culture and this time it will be my son who will live my dream. I enjoy observing my son's development into the German Culture. It has motivated him to become a good cook, be punctual, and even think and speak like a German. With our support he will succeed in becoming a trilingual adult,' explained Hanan.

With her abundance of balanced energy, Hanan runs her large villa, attends to her children and their extracurricular activities, and is a gracious hostess during the daily visits of her large extended family and friends.

Hanan's housekeeper assisted her in the kitchen while she cooked her traditional Emirati dishes for my cookbook. She enjoyed searching for fresh ingredients at her favourite stores in Al Ain. Hanan decided to prepare two favourite traditional Emirati drinks: *khambra*, also known as *habbel*, or *haba al hamra*, a drink with red cress seeds, and the second, *helba* made with fenugreek. Both drinks are often served to postpartum women. Nowadays however, adults and children also appreciate this comfort drink.

I drank Hanan's helba and admittedly it was delicious, smooth and comforting!

Helba

FENUGREEK BEVERAGE

SERVES 10–15

Hanan Rashid Hamdan Al Shookri said with a broad smile that *helba* is a smooth, warm, rich and creamy fenugreek beverage. In the Emirates and other Gulf countries, *helba* was traditionally drunk by mothers to stimulate lactation and boost recovery after childbirth. Today, *helba* is enjoyed by everyone.

½ cup fenugreek seeds
8 cups water (or more if needed)
¾ cup sweetened condensed milk (without cardamom flavour)
6 tbsp sugar (or more)
6 tbsp white flour
1 ½ cups water (will be mixed with flour)
1 tsp butter
2 tsp hand-rubbed zaatar
½ tsp ground black pepper
1 tsp cinnamon powder
1 tsp cardamom powder
1 pinch salt

Rinse fenugreek seeds until water runs clear. Add fenugreek seeds to 1 litre of water. Bring to a boil and reduce to medium heat. Continue stirring, making sure that seeds are always covered with water. Cook until seeds are soft and cooked but not mushy. This may take up to 1 hour. Add sugar, *zaatar*, pepper, cinnamon, cardamom and a pinch of salt and mix well. Add condensed milk and stir. Add flour to 1½ cups water, mix and add to pot. Stir to mix. Continue to cook fenugreek mixture until it has thickened slightly. Add butter and continue cooking for another 3 minutes. Pour mixture in a thermos. *Helba* will keep warm for several hours. Serve warm or at room temperature.

I drank haba al hamra at home in Al Bateen, Abu Dhabi in a relaxing environment with soft music playing in the background. I had a wonderful night's sleep. Try it!

Haba Al Hamra

SERVES 10–15

A smooth, creamy and rich beverage made with edible cress seeds. The cress seed, often called 'garden cress seed', belongs to the mustard family and has a mild peppery and pungent taste. *Haba al hamra* is traditionally served to postpartum women and guests coming to congratulate the new parents. It is also served during weddings and for Eid.

½ cup cress seeds
8 cups water
⅔ cup unsweetened condensed milk
½ cup sugar (or more)
6 tbsp instant custard powder
½ tsp black pepper, ground
1 pinch saffron powder
1 stick cinnamon
½ tsp cardamom powder
1 tsp vanilla extract

Rinse cress seeds until water runs clear. Soak cress seeds in ½ litre of water for 15 minutes. Rinse until water runs clear. Place cress seeds in a medium sized pot, add 1.5 litres of water, cinnamon stick and bring to a boil and simmer for 5 minutes. Whisk gently and skim off foam. Make sure that there are no lumps in the mixture. Continue stirring over medium heat to prevent mixture from sticking to the pot. Add cardamom, saffron, sugar and black pepper. Cook until mixture has thickened and has developed a gel-like consistency. Mix custard with condensed milk until creamy. Pour custard mixture into pot in 3 batches mixing well after each addition. Add vanilla and continue to stir for 2 minutes. Remove pot from the heat. Pour cooked haba al hamra into a thermos or into small teacups. Serve warm or at room temperature.

Mirat

SHEIKHA MOHAMED AL KAABI'S 'MEYLAS' FOOD TRUCK

ABU DHABI

'PEOPLE MAY FORGET WHAT I HAVE SAID BUT THEY WILL NEVER FORGET MY EMIRATI DISHES ONCE THEY HAVE TASTED THEM.'

Meeting Sheikha Mohammed Al Kaabi, a Masters graduate in Executive Business Administration from Sheikh Zayed University in Abu Dhabi, United Arab Emirates, was an exceptional experience for me.

33 year-old Sheikha Al Kaabi, a classic beauty of small and dainty build, is an innovative, hyper talented and passionate business lady and entrepreneur. She is from a noble and well-established Emirati family. In November 2014 she launched 'Meylas', the first Emirati food truck serving traditional Emirati cuisine.

Sheikha brings a new concept of eating appreciation to traditional Emirati dishes cooked and served directly from the truck to everyone who is curious about the taste of the exquisite cuisine of the United Arab Emirates. Sheikha's vision of her much anticipated 'Meylas' Restaurant became a reality on June 15, 2015!

You will often see Sheikha standing in front of the truck talking about traditional Emirati dishes and the importance of the packaging design in order to attract the younger Emirati generation as well as adults. She wants to share her passion for food and in doing so fill Emiratis with authentic pride for their local food culture.

Sheikha focuses on quality and freshness. All the dishes on the menu are made by hand. Often you will be served by Yussef from India, a very handsome young man who genuinely enjoys his position as the cook in Sheikha's Food Truck. Yussef's smile is addictive and you can tell that cooking Emirati traditional dishes is his passion! He has a typical Emirati appearance with a short, neatly trimmed beard. I asked Yussef if he was often mistaken for an Emirati and he proudly smiled and said: 'Yes and I enjoy it!' Sheikha makes sure that all her kitchen staff are dressed impeccably with clean, crisp, white uniforms and groomed hair.

Every dish, and I tasted most of them during both interviews with Sheikha, are big on flavours and the most popular dish is without a doubt the *legeimat* dish.

Legeimat is a lighter version of the North American one-bite doughnuts with a big difference ... they are made fresh within the food truck with natural ingredients, a twist of saffron, a light drizzle of date syrup and sprinkled with sesame seeds. Served warm, they are simply delectable!

When ordering a box of *legeimat* make sure to order a demi-cup (small cup) of their local coffee known as *qahwa*. Emirati coffee is taken without sugar or milk. *Qahwa* is a mixture of lightly roasted coffee beans and cardamom and mixed with powdered saffron. Don't miss this delightful combination of *legeimat* and *qahwa*! I know that you will not be able to stop until you have devoured all the *legeimat*!

Through her freshly made Emirati dishes, Sheikha wants to re-introduce and enlighten the Emiratis and all other cultures living, working and touring the United Arab Emirates about the importance of local food.

With a glitter in her eyes, Sheikha told me that she spent many days, nights and months with her mother and her mother's friends cooking, testing and retesting the pre-selected traditional Emirati dishes for her 'Meylas' Food Truck and eventually for her 'Meylas' Restaurant which officially opened June 15, 2015. 'I'm determined to raise the consciousness of our local dishes to everyone in the United Arab Emirates. I am very proud and passionate about Emirati food and culture and I want everyone to experience and share our local cuisine.'

Her artist friend Dana Mazroui, created the striking 'Meylas' truck logo making it visible from afar. 'I am even thinking of ordering a second truck from the United States which may take 3 months to arrive. After my team test the second food truck, we will be hiring new staff and they will be driving throughout the United Arab Emirates all the way to Fujairah Emirate.

During the interview she continued: 'New ideas keep surfacing and some of them I envision because they feel right. My new project is my 'Meylas' Restaurant which serves traditional Emirati dishes. The restaurant design is based on comfortable and classic ambient Arab décor. Guests will feel as if they are dining in an Emirati home. Eating at 'Meylas' will guarantee that the feel of Emirati hospitality will never be forgotten.'

Sheikha held my fascination: 'Our Emirati hospitality is an integral part of our food culture and I will be teaching my staff to transmit our hospitality. Food culture demands respect, appreciation and acknowledgment of everyone who is participating in the act of eating. This is why it is so very important for me to convey our traditional food culture through my food truck and restaurant concept nationally and internationally. I believe in my vision of the food truck and 'Meylas' Restaurant. They will be a most effective means to advance the news of our Emirati food culture to everyone!'

Part two for this interview took place in the back of a hotel in Abu Dhabi during a photo shoot for my book. She put on her kitchen gloves and prepared a fresh batch of *legeimat* for me. I was touched by her thoughtfulness considering that she had many interviews and photo shoots to attend. I considered myself very privileged. This is when I learned that when preparing *legeimat* a considerable amount of saffron has to be added in order to actually taste this heavenly spice, considered to be the 'gold spice', because it is the most expensive spice in the world.

If you have never tasted Emirati food or have not travelled to the United Arab Emirates, then it is time for you to make that very special trip and experience Sheikha's food truck 'Meylas' and taste your way through her exquisite menu! It is worth the trip! I would suggest that you contact Sheikha's office first to find out where her 'Meylas' Food Truck will be stationed the day you plan to be in the United Arab Emirates, as she changes location on a regular basis. You can also see the 'Meylas' Food Truck on Instagram: @meylas. Her truck graphics and matching packaging visuals are superb!

Sheikha Mohamed Al Kaabi's 'Meylas' Food Truck and newly opened restaurant can be explored by visiting *www.meylas.com*.

Batheetha

DATES WITH TOASTED FLOUR

SERVES 10–15

Batheetha is one of Sheikha's favourite sweet dishes that she learned from her mother and aunt. This traditional recipe incorporates pureed dates into the flour mixture.

1 kg whole wheat flour
1 tbsp Emirati ghee (clarified butter), melted
½ kg date paste
1 pinch saffron threads
1 tbsp sesame seeds
1 tbsp cardamom powder

Put flour in a heavy skillet or large pot and place on low heat. Stir flour constantly with a whisk to prevent burning! This process may take up to 1 hour for a dark brown colour. For a medium toast similar to light caramel colour it will take 7–10 minutes on medium heat. Remove toasted flour from skillet and allow it to cool for 5 minutes. Wash hands, you will be using your hands to mix the ingredients for each step of this recipe. Add date paste to toasted flour and mix with your hands until date paste is well incorporated in flour. Add melted Emirati ghee and cardamom to mixture. Add saffron and sesame seeds. Blend mixture well with your hands until the mixture resembles crumbs. Ready to be served!

I drank haba al hamra at home in Al Bateen, Abu Dhabi in a relaxing environment with soft music playing in the background. I had a wonderful night's sleep. Try it!

Legeimat

ONE-BITER MINI DOUGHNUTS

SERVES 6–8 DEPENDING ON SIZE

1 kg white flour
1 tbsp yeast (non-instant)
2 tbsp sugar
1 tbsp yoghurt
½ tbsp salt
1 pinch cardamom powder
1 pinch saffron threads
1¼ cup water
1½ tbsp date syrup
3 cups oil for frying

Using your hands mix all dry ingredients together in a large bowl until there are no lumps. Add water and knead with hands by stirring and alternatively beating with hands against the bowl until the dough is smooth and has become slightly liquid in consistency. This method of beating against the bowl is to make sure there are no lumps. Allow the dough to rest for approximately 1 hour in a warm place, or till doubled in size. Heat oil in a deep pan over medium heat. Using your thumb, index and middle fingers lift dough in small balls and drop into hot oil. Turn *legeimat* using a large metal spoon to get an even golden colour. Dip your fingers in water in between each *legeimat*. Once *legeimat* is ready, transfer to a large bowl and sprinkle with sesame seeds. Transfer *legeimat* to individual dishes and drizzle 1–2 tbsp date syrup per portion (one portion is approximately 5 *legeimat*).

Eat while they are still warm, they are to die for! And if you have a chance, visit Sheikha Al Kaabi's 'Meylas' Food Truck or her 'Meylas' Restaurant in Abu Dhabi for the best 'homemade' *legeimat* in town!

MARIAM ABDULLAH AL FALASI

DUBAI

FROM A BEDOUIN LIFE TO A LIFE IN A MANSION: MEET THE WOMAN WHO IS PLANNING HER OWN START-UP COMPANY.

On my way to my interviews in Jumeirah, Dubai, I decided to take the bus to gain travel experience. I got what I wished for: a bus driver with a unique style of driving! He applied the brakes every 2–3 kilometres while driving at 100 kilometres per hour. The driver insisted that it was necessary to apply the brakes and that, had he been in his native India, he would have driven the same way and applied the brakes even harder!

We finally arrived at our destination despite the constant stop and go. I walked to a nearby Indian restaurant where I ordered two cups of *karak* tea which calmed me. I called Mariam to request that she pick me up. She arrived and opened the door: 'Alexandra, welcome to Jumeirah! Come ride with me around the Mall where we own and sell real estate. We'll visit my large estate just behind the mall.'

Mariam, whose deep black eyes sparkle with curiosity, is a small, delightful and energetic woman. She was wearing a local abaya which is a long black robe worn with a hijab, a creatively wrapped black scarf covering the head and neck. Mariam wore a traditional but stunning Bedouin dress under her abaya.

To my surprise most of the interview took place while she drove. She told me that her Bedouin mother belonged to the Al Falasi tribe while her father hailed from the Tamin tribe. She proudly added that H.H. Mohammed bin Rashid Al Maktoum, Ruler of Dubai, was a descendant of the House of Al Falasi and its leader. We arrived at her mansion, complete with underground garage, accommodating her family, two of her sons' families and her other five children.

Upon our arrival in one of her many welcoming *majlis*, Mariam prepared freshly squeezed orange juice which she served with fresh dates. She asked me to choose from amongst 100 colourful head scarves to cover my head and neck. She would do the same, simply because there were many men from her family who would come and greet us in the welcoming area.

We continued our interview and Mariam proudly said: 'I became a mother when I was very young. I was fifteen. I have seven children and I made sure that they all have degrees and are in well paid positions. In the meantime, I learned to speak English by watching English television channels; this was my hobby for a long time until I was able to speak well.'

'However, the time has come for me to turn my passion into a business,' said Mariam with a charismatic smile. She explained: 'I have over 100 bottles of coconut oils infused with spices and fragrances that even the Queen of Sheba would have used: saffron, flower petals, herbs, spices, fragrances, herbal oils and flower oils. I will be branding my products next year after I have sold all one hundred bottles.' Then Mariam stood up energetically and recommended that we go to the kitchen to start cooking her favourite recipes. The day went by quickly.

The bus driver returning to Abu Dhabi was only able to drive at 50–75 kilometre per hour due to unforeseen technical problems. It took us five hours instead of two to reach Abu Dhabi. This was indeed a day filled with unexpected adventures!

Mamshoora Maleh

SHREDDED SALTED FISH SALAD WITH RICE

SERVES 6–8

2 cups maleh (salted fish)
2 tomatoes, cubed
1 onion, peeled and thinly sliced
1 large lemon, cut into small cubes (remove seeds)
1⅓ water cups water
2 small green chillies, chopped and deseeded
2 tbsp coriander, chopped
2 tbsp parsley, chopped

Rinse salted fish under cold water for 1 minute. Skin and debone fish. Place fish in a large bowl and cover with cold water. Soak for 30 minutes. Remove fish from bowl, discard water and rinse under cold water for 1 minute. Place rinsed fish back in bowl, again cover with cold water and leave to soak for another 30 minutes. Remove fish from water and pat dry. Using your hands shred fish into small pieces (do not use a food processor). In a medium sized bowl add shredded fish and the remainder of the ingredients. Using your hands squeeze the ingredients in the bowl for 1 full minute. Mix, cover and marinate for 30 minutes in the refrigerator. Serve shredded fish salad with rice. Use rice recipe from this chapter.

Mariam Abdullah Al Falasi's mamshoora maleh or Shredded Salted Fish Salad has a fragrant and fresh lemony flavour that tastes heavenly!

Mariam Abdullah Al Falasi's recipes are labour intensive but are a must for anyone who is curious and adventurous! The flavours that develop during the cooking process are highly addictive palate pleasers!

Maleh

SERVES UP TO 30

1 large, clean plastic bucket with lid
10 medium-sized mackerels
2 kg organic coarse sea salt or more
½ kg fresh whole green chilli peppers
10 limes, sliced
10 sticks cassia
1 cup *bzar* (see page 15)

METHOD AND BUTTERFLY CUTTING TECHNIQUE:

Remove tail, fins and gut the mackerel. Do not wash, discard head. Place fish on cutting board and make an incision from the belly to the head, all the way to the backbone, but not right through. Unfold fish and lay it skin-side down on a large platter. Butterfly remaining fish. Put a 3 cm thick layer of coarse salt on the bottom of the clean bucket. Layer butterflied fish skin-side down next to each other. Add another 3 cm thick layer of salt over fish. Continue layering all the butterflied fish, skin side down with 3 cm coarse salt until all the fish is covered with salt. Top with green chilli peppers, limes, cassia and *bzar*. Cover bucket and let rest for 1–6 month. After a few days the salt will have extracted water from the fish. Check weekly to ensure that the fish is submerged in brine. If not, add more salt. Do not add water!

Tahta Maleh

SALTED FISH WITH RICE

SERVES 4–6

INGREDIENTS FOR SALOONA MALEH OR SPICY SAUCE WITH SALTED FISH:

250 g maleh (salted fish)
¼ cup vegetable oil
2 *loumi*, crushed and seeded (dried limes)
1 bay leaf, broken into pieces
2 large onions, peeled and sliced
3 garlic cloves, peeled and chopped
2 green chilli peppers, seeded and chopped
1 tsp whole cumin
1 tsp cardamom powder
1 tbsp *bzar* (see page 15)
½ tsp chilli peppers, flaked
½ cup coriander, chopped
½ cup parsley, chopped

INGREDIENTS FOR RICE:

3 cups basmati rice
12 cups water (or more)
2 tsp salt
1 tbsp vegetable oil
½ tsp saffron threads, soaked in a little in water (optional)
3 tbsp coriander, chopped
3 tbsp parsley, chopped

Rinse salted fish under cold water for 1 minute. Skin and debone fish. Place fish in a large bowl and cover with cold water. Soak for 30 minutes. Remove fish from bowl, discard water and rinse under cold water for 1 minute. Place rinsed fish back in bowl, again cover with cold water and leave to soak for another 30 minutes. Remove fish from water and pat dry. Using your hands shred fish into small pieces (do not use a food processor). Heat oil in a medium-sized saucepan over medium heat, add onions, garlic, cardamom, crushed *loumi* and *bzar*. Cook until onion is translucent and spices begin to smell fragrant. Add all remaining ingredients except coriander and parsley. Stir until you begin to smell the fragrance of the newly added spices. Add coriander and parsley, mix, remove from heat, cover and set aside until ready to be layered into the rice dish.

RICE:

Rinse rice until water runs clear. Soak rice in cold water for 30 minutes. Drain. Bring water to a boil. Add rice and salt. Bring to a boil, reduce heat and simmer until rice is 50 % cooked. To test for 50 % doneness, squeeze grain between your thumb and index finger. You should feel a semi-hard center. Drain rice completely. Add oil to the pot to prevent rice from sticking. Place half the rice back into the pot and cover with prepared spicy sauce and fish.

Do not mix.

Top with remaining rice, sprinkle with coriander and parsley. Pour saffron over rice (optional). Cover and cook rice at very low heat until it is fully cooked and tender. Spoon tahta maleh into a large serving dish or serve from pot.

HALIMA AL ATTAR
FUJAIRAH

'MY EIGHT CHILDREN, MY HUSBAND AND MY DEEP CAKE COMPANY.'

I met Halima Al Attar while visiting the 2014 'Dubai World Hospitality Championships'. This international competition organization falls under the directives of His Highness Sheikh Hamdan bin Mohammed bin Rashid Al Maktoum, Crown Prince of Dubai. I decided to walk over to Halima's stand which was laden with beautifully displayed cupcakes and Emirati sweets.

I introduced myself to Halima, her daughters and her friend. I casually asked if she wanted to be part of my book. She looked at me, paused and asked: 'Would you come all the way to Fujairah?' We both laughed and arranged for a suitable interview date.

I was grateful that my friend Azza Al Qubaisi invited me to stay with her in Fujairah. The following day we decided to take the car in search of Halima's residence. To my dismay we encountered three homes where the ladies of the homes all had the same first name, 'Halima'! We were later told that they were all related to Halima Al Attar.

Halima introduced herself and explained that she and her husband were cousins, which is not uncommon amongst Emirati families. They also have the same last name 'Al Attar' and belong to the 'Al Attar' tribe from Fujairah.

Halima is through and through a kind-hearted woman surrounded by an aura of harmony. I was invited to sit and watch as Halima and her daughters prepared a variety of dishes for the interview and for our welcome. Her kitchen table was covered with various cupcakes, biscuits, dates, fruits, milk, freshly pressed watermelon juice, tea, Emirati coffee and chocolate covered candy. Although I had had breakfast before coming to the interview, I must have given the impression that I had not eaten for days: I tested every dish!

I commented on the great teamwork between Halima and her daughters. She confirmed: 'The relationship between myself and my four daughters can only be understood by mothers and daughters. We work together harmoniously and what remains constant is our unconditional love for one another. This unconditional support helped me win the Emirati Gold traditional food award during the 2014 'Dubai World Hospitality Championships'.' It was awarded in the 'Emirati Amateur Chefs' category and I won it on behalf of my Deep Cake Co. catering company.

Halima continued with her story: 'My catering company, Deep Cake Co., has only become a success due to our team work. It is a fusion of traditional, contemporary and international cuisine mixed with creative and savoury Emirati dishes. And it's all prepared in my garden under the great blue sky. Cupcakes, cookies, cakes and gifts for celebrations and corporate events are prepared inside my home.'

'When you find something that you are passionate about, develop it and your passion will be rewarded with success!' exclaimed Halima with inspired conviction.

'I raised eight children, four girls and four boys, all without a housekeeper. I taught my children to look after themselves. In doing so, my children became independent and started their own lives with confidence. When I started my company two years ago, I decided to hire a housekeeper for our large home. However, I still prepare family dishes three times a day and cook for my clients. Every meal is different but it's mostly Emirati!'

'My husband and my children created a wonderful environment which is conducive to creative cooking and baking. This is very rewarding for a mother. One of my daughters is currently studying business administration in Al Ain, Abu Dhabi, and has become our company accountant. Another daughter in Al Ain is our designer and marketer and the other two are also studying. Their passion is cooking and baking.'

'I am always aware that I can absolutely trust and count on my family's support,' said Halima. 'My daughters and I enjoy cooking traditional and contemporary dishes. Our clients appreciate the exquisite cuisine that we create as a team. We delight in transmitting our love of cooking to others!' exclaimed Halima with pride.

Jasheed

SHARK FISH IN SPICY TOMATO SAUCE WITH RICE

SERVES 6–8

While Halima was cooking during the interview she explained: 'I am using my mother's *jasheed* recipe. The one that she received from her mother. In the United Arab Emirates, *jasheed* is mainly eaten by the older generation. This dish is simple and easy to follow and it is amazingly delicious!"

INGREDIENTS FOR JASHEED:

- 2 kg shark
- 8 cups water (or more if required)
- 1 tbsp salt

INGREDIENTS FOR SPICY JASHEED SAUCE:

- 1 cup water (or more if required)
- ½ cup vegetable oil
- 4 onions, peeled and cubed
- 4 medium tomatoes, cubed
- 4 *loumi*, crushed (dried limes)
- 1 tbsp *sheenea* (curly grey-bluish mushrooms found in the mountains of Fujairah or use dried mushrooms of your choice)
- 2 tbsp salt
- 1 garlic bulb, peeled and chopped
- ⅓ cup tomato paste
- 6 green chilli peppers, seeded and chopped
- 1 stick cassia (1 inch), broken into small pieces
- 1 tbsp ground black pepper
- 1 tbsp coriander powder
- 2 tbsp turmeric powder
- 1 tsp chilli peppers, dried and flaked
- 2 tbsp oregano
- 2 tbsp fresh mint, chopped
- 1 tbsp cumin powder
- ½ cup fresh coriander, chopped

INGREDIENTS FOR RICE:

- 2 kg basmati rice
- 8 cups water
- 2 tbsp salt
- 1 cup fresh coriander, chopped

Purchase shark from a reputable fishmonger who will sell you a freshly caught shark. Sharks must be thoroughly cleaned to remove odour. Cut the cleaned shark into 2 cm slices. In a large pot bring water to boil, add salt and shark slices. Cover and cook on medium heat for 30 minutes or until soft in texture. Make sure the shark meat is submerged in the boiling water. Remove from heat and cool in the fish water. When cool, remove skin and bones and place in a bowl, cover and set aside

SPICY JASHEED SAUCE:

Heat oil in large, heavy saucepan over medium heat. Add onions and 3 green chillies. Stir and cook until onions are translucent. Add the other 3 green chilli peppers, tomatoes, garlic, *loumi* and tomato paste. Stir and cook until tomatoes start to soften and break down. Add ¼ cup water, stir and continue cooking for 5 minutes. Add another ¼ cup water and prepared shark meat and stir. Add all remaining spices except cumin powder and fresh coriander. Mash shark meat in sauce, add another ¼ cup water, mix and stir until spices exude an aromatic spicy fragrance. Continue to mash shark meat with fork until it has become a puree-like consistency. Add cumin powder. Simmer for about 20 minutes or until sauce thickens. Taste and adjust spices.

Note: Sauce is very spicy. Continue stirring until spices exude an aromatic spicy fragrance, if you adjusted spices. Add another ¼ cup water and simmer until sauce has thickened once again. Remove from heat and cover to keep warm. Before serving, garnish with fresh coriander.

RICE:

Rinse basmati rice until water runs clear. Soak for 30 minutes in cold water. Drain. Add rice and salt to boiling water. Bring to boil and turn heat off. Rice will continue to cook. Steam rice until done. Check for doneness while cooking. Bite into a grain of rice or do as the Emiratis do: squeeze rice grain between your thumb and index finger. The rice is done when the grain is tender. Drain rice completely. Arrange rice on large serving platter and garnish with chopped coriander. Spoon *jasheed* sauce on a serving platter, garnish with fresh coriander and serve with rice.

Bedouin Camel Milk and Date Smoothie

SERVES 4

'Camel milk with dates is a perfect breakfast meal. Bedouins long survived in the desert drinking warm camel milk with dates. Today, I make delicious camel milk and date smoothies for my family and for my clients.'

2 cups cold or warm camel milk
7 fresh Medjool dates

Combine camel milk and pitted dates. Blend until smooth. Serve immediately or store in an airtight container in the refrigerator.

CHEF KHULOOD ATIQ
DUBAI

FIRST FEMALE EMIRATI CELEBRITY CHEF

Six months into my cookbook research and interviews, I was finally able to meet the 'First Female Emirati Celebrity Chef': Chef Khulood Atiq at the 'Emirati Kitchen' event. Chef Atiq had already impressed me with her Emirati cookbook 'Sarareed' which was produced in collaboration with the Abu Dhabi Tourism Development and Investment Company (TDIC). It was launched on 9 February 2012 at the Armed Forces Club and Hotel during the 'Gourmet Abu Dhabi 2012', a premier culinary festival celebrating the most renowned chefs in the United Arab Emirates.

Beautiful, charming with an energetic personality, Chef Atiq is considered one of the rising stars amongst the culinary world at home in the Emirates and internationally with her dishes like *balaleet*, *machbous*, Emirati pickles and many other dishes that are an essential part of Emirati cuisine. The three recipes that I chose from Chef Atiq's cookbook, *balaleet* (sweet rice noodle dish with scrambled eggs), *shorbat adas* (lentil soup) and *harees* soup (savoury porridge soup) will turn you into an ardent fan of this exceptional chef's recipes.

This is what Chef Atiq said about her book: 'The book involves more than just recipes. It highlights the Emirati culture as well as the cuisine. It confirms Emirati traditions of hospitality as receiving and honouring guests with enormous generosity, which is considered a crucial part of Emirati heritage. It also features fascinating insights into how these recipes were developed.'

Emirati hospitality is something that all of us can learn from. 'Receiving and honouring' as Atiq said, is the fundamental foundation of family bonding, a tradition that Emirati Bedouins have passed on to their children. Emiratis perfected the art of honouring and receiving their family and guests. I had the pleasure of witnessing this revered tradition when families eat together, sitting on the floor around the *sarrut*, a large round mat on which dishes are placed in a circle to accommodate every person.

Chef Atiq revealed the importance of establishing Emirati food awareness to everyone living and working in the United Arab Emirates as well as outside the Emirates because she believes in developing and preserving the Emirati food culture. Chef Atiq introduced Emirati food awareness through her cookbook 'Sarareed', television cooking shows, interviews, live shows and events.

While I was chatting with Chef Atiq and preparing to photograph her for my cookbook, she was hosting her own cooking show at the 'Emirati Kitchen' event which took place along The Corniche (Road) in Abu Dhabi. She asked me with her charming and enigmatic smile: 'Alexandra, am I beautiful?' I answered emphatically: 'You are indeed beautiful Khulood!' I enjoyed photographing her because she connected with the camera while explaining her recipe to her expat audience.

Chef Atiq, born March 21, 1983 and raised in Dubai, is a celebrity Chef in the United Arab Emirates, as well as a consultant for the Abu Dhabi Tourism Development and Investment Company. She is always very excited about Emirati food culture being presented to expats, visitors, Emiratis living in and outside the United Arab Emirates.

Her inspiration for becoming a cook was none other than her mother whom she watched every Friday preparing dough to bake traditional Emirati bread. Her mother patiently taught her the art of cooking Emirati dishes which became a lifelong passion for her*.

Chef Atiq does not rule out opening her own restaurant at some point in the future and has her heart set on being awarded the famous 'Michelin Award'. Atiq is happiest eating at home. 'Friday is family day,' she says. 'Gathering with the entire family while we cook and eat is something I hold very close to my heart.'

The recipes in this chapter have been reproduced in their entirety and without alteration with the permission of Chef Khulood Atiq, from her Emirati cuisine cookbook Sarareed.

Balaleet Dish

1 box of thin noodles
1 small onion cut into thin pieces (optional)
2 tablespoons of ghee
½–¾ cup of sugar
1 tsp cardamom powder
1 tsp saffron
3 eggs

Boil water in a pot then add to it the noodles with 1 tablespoon of ghee, and continue boiling for 2 minutes. Drain the noodles and add the sugar to them while still hot in order for the sugar to melt. Add 2 tablespoons of ghee to the same pot used earlier in order to fry the onion and then add the eggs to this and stir the mixture. Stir the cardamom and saffron into the noodles and then put this in the pot with the eggs and place it in the oven on medium heat for 5 minutes. Keep the pot closed until the liquid evaporates.

Chef's Note: Some people simply fry eggs and put it on the thin noodles before serving. The use of onions is optional.

The original recipe ingredients are as noted. During the cooking demonstration with the author, Chef Khulood Atiq used 200 grams of Rice Vermicelli noodles.

Shorbat Adas

TRADITIONAL LENTIL SOUP

'Lentil Soup is a favourite amongst the natives of the Arabian Gulf, especially in winter as it keeps them warm. It is easily prepared and contains very few ingredients, including the ever-delicious *loumi* (dried lime).'

These recipes have been reproduced in their entirety and without alteration, by permission from Chef Khulood Atiq's Emirati cuisine cookbook *Sarareed*.

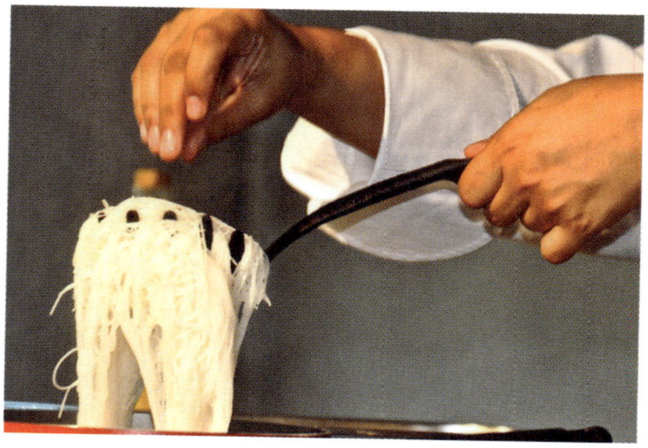

Harees Soup

WHEAT SOUP

'This is "indirectly" made while cooking the *harees* dish. It consists of the remaining water that floats on top of the well-cooked *harees* (wheat) with a little portion of meat added to it. Over time, people started making this soup separately without cooking the main *harees* dish.'

1 cup *harees* (wheat)
500 g meat or chicken (boiled)
2 l water
salt
2 *loumi* (dried lime)

Wash the *harees* (wheat) and soak it in water for an hour. In a pot, cook the meat or chicken in hot water until it boils. Put the *harees* (wheat) and the salt in a pot, cover it, and cook it for approximately 3 hours until it is well-cooked. Blend the *harees* soup, or serve it the traditional way. Perforate the *loumi* before adding it to the soup to help the flavours seep through. Serve it hot.

Chef's Remark: Chopped vegetables can be used to enhance the flavour and nutritional value of the soup.

1 cup washed yellow lentils
1 finely chopped onion
1 l water
½ tsp ground cumin
½ tsp curry powder
1 tbsp ground black pepper
1 pinch of salt (or as desired)
2 *loumi* (dried lime)
1 tbsp chopped coriander
2 tbsp ghee

Heat the ghee or oil in a pot. Add the chopped onion and cook, stirring frequently, until it browns. Add the lentil, salt and spices to the pot and stir for a while. Add hot water to the pot and leave the mixture to boil for 40 minutes until the lentils are cooked. Add the *loumi* and coriander to the mix and let the soup boil until it thickens. Serve while hot.

CHEF MUSABBEH AL KAABI
DUBAI

THE FIRST EMIRATI FOOD CHEF IN THE UAE

I met Chef Musabbeh Al Kaabi, the first Emirati food chef, shortly before I flew back to Berlin in 2015. This meeting was one of the major highlights during my eighteen-month search for Emirati men and women for contributions to my Emirati cookbook.

Chef Musabbeh's culinary career started after serving seven years in the United Arab Emirates Army forces. In 2001, he joined Jebel Ali International Hotels Golf Resort & Spa as Commis Chef, then went to the Oasis Beach Hotel until 2005. In 2006, Chef Musabbeh joined the Jumeirah Group where he worked three years at Jumeirah Beach Hotel.

In 2009, he became Sous Chef De Cuisine at the Dubai World Trade Centre and then became the Head Chef in the Kempinski Hotel Mall of the Emirates. Chef Musabbeh then became a Concept Consultant Chef for the pre-opening of Shawati restaurant in Abu Dhabi before moving to the Cassels hotel in Al Barsha where he was an Executive Chef.

Prior to joining Jumeirah Zabeel Saray in 2011, Chef Musabbeh was famous for his Ramadan cooking shows which were featured on both Kuwaiti Channel Al Rai TV segment 'Sufra Khaleejeeya' and Sharjah TV segment 'Cooking and More'. To this day, Musabbeh still presents various TV shows and cooking demonstrations across the region including the United Arab Emirates Culinary Competition and programs for Jumeirah in the USA.

Chef Al Kaabi added that he and his team won the Gold Medal for the Emirati Culinary Competition during the 2013 and 2014 Dubai World Hospitality Championships held at the Dubai World Trade Centre under the directive of His Highness Sheikh Hamdan Bin Mohammed Al Maktoum, Crown Prince of Dubai. This gifted premier Chef will surely be the recipient of many more culinary awards to come!

Chef Al Kaabi arranged to have the interview in the hotel lobby of the Jumeirah Zabeel Saray in the West Crescent Palm Jumeirah in Dubai where he works as the Executive Oriental Chef. He welcomed me in true Emirati hospitality and culture with an array of petit fours, mixed nuts, local dates, Emirati tea and coffee, water and fruits. It was of no surprise as Emiratis are masters in the art of welcoming their guests! I felt welcomed, honoured and acknowledged.

Chef Al Kaabi is an influential food expert and exercises leadership with kindness. I noted that Chef Musabbeh had a tremendous amount to contribute from his vast knowledge and experience with Emirati traditional dishes. In his confident and focused 'savoir-faire' he confided: 'As a nation we Emiratis love to eat and enjoy sharing our homemade traditional Emirati dishes with our families and guests. When the team and I cook my Emirati creations, I do it thinking of the guests and so I take special care in the selection of fresh foods. I also respect my cooking team: after all, they prepare the food! Alexandra, I love my country and I wish to inspire everyone interested in the continuity of our traditional Emirati food culture.'

He stressed the importance of consuming fresh organic produce: 'Our traditional Emirati dishes are prepared with organic fruits and vegetables which result in high quality, healthy dishes with authentic flavours and fragrances. This is vital for the authenticity and sustainability of our traditional Emirati dishes.'

Chef Al Kaabi reminisced that he became aware and fond of food as a young boy, barely five years old, living with his family in Hatta, a city in Abu Dhabi half-way between Al Ain and the island of Abu Dhabi.

His father often took him on a four day camel ride to Dubai in scorching heat in order to sell the 'charcoal' prepared by his father. The 'charcoal', from the samar tree and tobacco leaves, was hung to dry for three days and then cured by smoking and drying in a pan over gentle flames which brought out the natural sweet taste in the tobacco. When cooled down the tobacco was ready to be used for water pipes known as 'shisha' in exchange for fish, sugar and preserved meat.

Chef Al Kaabi continued to describe his experience and connection with traditional Emirati dishes through his mother's influence while she cooked and through his father who showed him the importance of harvesting only the best quality and mature produce for superior flavour and aroma. This seems to have fascinated him. Proudly he said: 'By nature I am still a farmer!'

While Chef Al Kaabi was savouring black tea and the delicious marzipan-like consistency of local dates known as *maamoul* and *khoudry*, he reflected that from 1981–1982 the Hatta Fort was being constructed by Indian Sikhs. As a young boy he and his father would deliver, twice a week, basic food staples for the Indian construction workers: yellow dates, limes, tomatoes, onion, garlic, mangoes, seasonal and sweet potatoes. All this produce was grown on their family farm in Hatta.

When I asked Chef Al Kaabi what it would take for the younger and future generations to be interested in their own traditional dishes, he replied: 'I have observed that men and women identify with their traditional food and etiquette culture once they have married and have had children. That is when they focus on settling down and teaching their children traditional and modern values. Children cause parents to become emotional which often results in re-establishing the importance of family, traditional food and cultural traditions.

The first and most important aspect of our food culture is that we connect the act of sharing food with our eating etiquette, meaning that while we sit on the floor and eat around a large platter of food, we respect the area on the platter from which each person eats. Each person has his or her area to eat from the platter, and if the meat portion happens to be on the other side of the platter, he or she must ask permission to have the piece of meat in question. We also bless the food before eating which is a ritual that grounds us and calms us down after a stressful day.

It's important to note that the most popular spices used in our food culture are saffron and cardamom while the most popular dishes for each Emirate, and I would like to start with Abu Dhabi, is, in my opinion the *tahta* rice dish. In Fujairah it is the fish *machbous*, in Umm Al Quwain the *maleh* salted fish, in Sharjah it would be *nakhi* and in all other Emirates it would be the well-known dish *biryani* which originated from the Indian *biryani*.

In the United Arab Emirates most families have their own spice mixture recipe used for traditional dishes. We call this mixture *bzar*. In my family, our *bzar* is composed of over ten spices, and the dominant note is the clove. Each family has their recognizable note in their *bzar*. Often you will be able to buy Emirati *bzar* with personal notes and fragrances from our traditionally dressed women who wear the facial mask, known as *burqa*. They are beautiful women who enjoy preparing and selling their own *bzar* at one of the local markets. This generates supplemental income for them.

I will give you some of my favourite traditional recipes for your book. I know your readers will enjoy preparing and enjoying the finished product, provided that they are made with love and passion! The saffron and milk drink *halib jaman* and *muhlabia*, a sweet camel milk rice pudding can easily be made in your own kitchen,' promised the brilliant chef.

Muhallabia is making a real comeback in the Emirates. Eating it brings back fond memories of one's childhood. It truly is comfort food at its best.

Muhallabia

RICE PUDDING WITH CAMEL MILK, SAFFRON AND CARDAMOM

SERVES 6–8

1 cup rice
6 cups camel milk
1½ cups sugar
½ tsp saffron threads
½ tsp ground cardamom

Rinse rice until water runs clear. Soak rice in cold water for 30 minutes. Drain and transfer to a large pot. Heat camel milk and transfer into the rice pot. Cook on low heat until rice is almost cooked, stirring occasionally. When rice is almost cooked, add saffron, cardamom and sugar. Cook for another 5 minutes or until rice is done, set aside and cool. Spoon pudding into serving bowls and garnish with a pinch of cardamom and saffron. Refrigerate until ready to be served.

Halib Jamal

CAMEL MILK WITH SAFFRON AND CARDAMOM

SERVES 6–8

6 cups camel milk
1 tsp saffron threads
7 cardamom pods

In a large pot add camel milk and bring to a boil. Add saffron and cardamom pods and simmer for 5 minutes. Cool until it is warm. Strain and serve.

Halib Jamal is simple to make yet delicious and soothing!

Bzar

EMIRATI SPICE MIX

This recipe is specially designed by Chef Musabbeh Al Kaabi for the *camel ghouzy* recipe. It is based on his mother's traditional *bzar* recipe.

75 g cumin seeds, ground
600 g black pepper, ground
250 g paprika powder
100 g coriander seeds, ground
100 g cloves, ground
100 g nutmeg, ground
100 g cinnamon sticks, ground
100 g cardamom powder
75 g bay leaves, ground
2.5 kg turmeric powder

Preheat oven at 160°C. Cover cookie sheet with parchment paper. Lightly dry-roast all spices in the oven for 10 minutes. Remove from oven and cool for 30 minutes. Store the ground spices in an airtight container away from light. This *bzar* spice mix can be stored for up to one year. Add this *bzar* to your recipes to impart a 'local' flavour.

Bedouin Camel Ghouzy

SERVES 30–40

Bedouin *camel ghouzy* is cooked in a very large pot, which includes an interior rack strainer over an open fire and served with rice.

INGREDIENTS FOR CAMEL GHOUZY:

1 young camel (approx. 1.5 years old dromedary or Arabian) (50–70 kg)
1 kg turmeric powder
1.8 kg salt
2.5 kg *bzar* (see page 129)
fresh coriander to garnish

Cut camel into large portion. Discard camel's head and all internal organs, except liver. Refrigerate liver for later use. Mix salt and turmeric and rub into the camel's carcass inside and out. Leave to penetrate through the skin for 1 hour. This ensures the removal of the remaining blood and odour from the freshly cut camel. After 1 hour, rinse camel portions with a hose until water runs clear.

Dry the meat and cut into smaller serving pieces. Prepare wood and charcoal fire in sand. Bring to a low fire and prepare embers which will be used during the last stage of cooking to brown meat. Place meat in large, clean basin and rub in *bzar* mixture. Cover and marinate for 3 hours in large refrigerator. Take a very large cooking pot with a round rack designed to accommodate 75 kg of meat and place on the fire. Place marinated meat on rack inside the pot.

Add water in pot from the side until ¾ full below meat. Water should not touch meat. Cover. This method will steam the camel meat and allow it to 'sweat' the water from the muscles. In turn this will keep meat tender. Cook for approximately 6 hours. Check every 30 minutes, adding water if necessary to prevent meat juices from burning. After 5½ hours, test meat for tenderness, then in the last stage of cooking place embers on top of lid and leave it for ½ hour to brown and colour the meat. Make sure there are no flames under the pot!

Set aside 1 litre of camel juice to cook rice!

INGREDIENTS FOR RICE:

15 kg basmati rice
250 g cardamom pods
250 g bay leaves
¼ cup cinnamon sticks, broken
salt, to taste
ground black pepper, to taste
38 l water
4 cups camel juice
fresh coriander to garnish

RICE:

Soak rice in salted water for 30 minutes. Make sure you start soaking the rice 1 hour before camel is finished cooking! Drain rice and transfer to large covered pot. Add salt and spices. Add water and the 1 litre of camel juice. This will add that distinct camel flavour. Bring to a boil and simmer until rice is cooked. Drain excess water if necessary. Serve camel on several large platters. Rice will be served on separate platters. Garnish rice and camel with coriander.

CHEF'S NOTE:

During our interview Chef Al Kaabi told me: 'Camel meat is a perfect example of how quality ingredients, prepared simply, make for something festive, even for our special Emirati occasions or holiday dinners. My mother always prepared a camel meal for our family and friends. Today, I pass this tradition on to my children.'

Then Chef Al Kaabi explained: '*Camel ghouzy* is considered to be a symbol of hospitality. It is served with many side dishes, bread, a variety of pickles as well as our delicacy: green radish tails or *rowaid* in Arabic.'

He continued to elaborate the importance of washing hands just before sharing a meal with family and guests, and to pray 'in the name of Allah' or '*bismillah*'.

'Emirati traditional dishes are very important to us because we consider food to have a sanctity of its own. It's considered to be Allah's most important gift to humankind,' he added.

CHEF LATIFA MASOOD

RAS AL KHAIMAH

'WHEN I FOLLOW MY INTUITION, I NEVER FEEL THAT I AM WORKING.'

I met Chef Latifa in Ras Al Khaimah, a city in northern coastal United Arab Emirates. Towards the end of our interview, I realized that Chef Latifa Masood was the person I had seen cooking on YouTube. I had been searching for her for one and a half years for my Emirati cookbook! I was sitting in her *majlis* not realizing that she was THE 'Chef Latifa'.

Latifa was born in 1983. Her mother, a slender and elegant person, was born and raised in Giza, Egypt. Her father was Emirati from the 'Masood' tribe and born and raised in Ras Al Khaimah.

Chef Latifa's mother was her most inspiring and motivational cook. She noticed, that her daughter had a God given gift for baking and cooking. 'I have always felt the urge to be creative and I found the medium through which my passion could be reflected: baking and cooking. While watching my mother baking her Egyptian bread in our traditional oven in the garden, I had joyful visions of myself baking and cooking traditional Emirati masterpieces.

This feeling of joy has not left me. When I observe my clients and friends connecting to my work, I realize that those are the moments in my life that I enjoy the most. I know that I have chosen the right path,' the passionate cook admits.

Chef Latifa decided to become a graphic designer and graduated from the School of Graphic Design in Ras Al Khaimah. After being chosen to become the pastry chef on Chef Khulood's television show in Abu Dhabi, Latifa participated in baking and cooking competitions and was honoured by Mohammed bin Rashid Al Maktoum, Vice President, Prime Minister of the United Arab Emirates and Ruler of Dubai.

Chef Latifa continued enthusiastically: 'After my graduation, I decided to turn my passion into a home business. Unfortunately, my father passed away and I became the sole earner for our family. I decided to work for the Ministry of Education during the day and follow my passion in the evenings and on weekends.'

During our interview, Chef Latifa explained that her food creations reflect her energy and passion: 'I observed that when I sell or give my products to my clients and friends, these creations foster a sense of honour, respect and connection! It is the same joy I felt when I was a young girl watching my mother bake her traditional Egyptian breads.'

'I would say that my cakes and sweets reflect modern clean lines with a fusion of classical strong colours, and maintain the required elegance that my clients expect. I also love to design elegant and fun theme events not to mention wedding cakes that I top with buttercream flowers, text, pictures, my own intricate or simple detail designs or those of the client.

When I asked Chef Latifa what her business will look like in five years, she replied with a twinkle in her eye: 'In five years I will have my own pastry chef television program, I will have my own kitchen with personally selected baking and cooking teams and I will manage my own online order platform in Ras Al Khaimah.'

I know that Chef Latifa is a great and gifted cook. I wish her the best and hope that all her dreams come true!

Achaar Tamat

TOMATO PICKLES

SERVES 10–12

Emiratis enjoy eating *achaar tamat* or tomato pickles with Emirati starters. Bread dunked in achaar *tamat* is so delicious that you may end up dunking the bread until the jar is empty! *Achaar tamat* is also eaten with rice and meat dishes.

500 g half-ripe red tomatoes
⅓ cup wild dried garlic, sliced (or 4 large garlic cloves and bake at lowest temperature until dry)
1 cup large crystal salt (also known as kosher salt)
1 tbsp coriander powder
2 garlic cloves, peeled
¼ cup round chilli peppers, dried
1½ cups white vinegar
2 large limes

Cut tomatoes into thick slices. Cut limes lengthwise into quarters. In medium-sized bowl, mix tomatoes, limes and salt. Place ⅓ mixture in sterilized jar, add ⅓ dried wild garlic slices and press hard. Repeat this process twice with the remaining mixture. Pour enough vinegar to cover. Top with fresh garlic cloves and red round chilli peppers. Seal jar and set outside under the sun for 10 days.

Achaar Liamun

LIME PICKLES

SERVES 10–12

5 organic limes
4 tbsp freshly squeezed lime juice
1 tbsp nigella seeds
1 cup large crystal salt (also known as kosher salt)
3 tbsp safflower threads
2–3 chilli peppers
½ cup white vinegar

Fill a saucepan with water and bring to a boil. Add 5 limes and cook until they have changed to a medium dark yellow colour. Remove from heat and cool at room temperature. Cut cooked limes into quarters but not through the base. They will become lemon flowers. Mix safflower, 2 tbsp kosher salt and the lime juice in a bowl. Fill the quartered limes with safflower mixture. Place filled limes into sterilized jar and top with chillies. Pour enough vinegar to cover the limes and chillies. Seal and set aside for 2 weeks in a dark, cool area.

Achaar Hamba

GREEN MANGO PICKLES

SERVES 10–12

Emiratis enjoy eating *achaar hamba* or mango pickles at virtually every main meal. It is especially tasteful when mixed into fish stew! *Achaar hamba* is served to complement any rice and stew dishes. In fact, pickles are considered a staple in the Emirati cuisine.

1 kg unripe Emirati or Indian mangos
2 tsp turmeric powder
2 tbsp corn oil
1 tbsp mustard seeds
1 cup vinegar
2 tbsp large salt crystals (also known as kosher salt)
4 red or green chilli peppers
1 tbsp nigella seeds
4 tbsp freshly squeezed lime juice

Peel, pit, quarter and slice mangos in thin slices. In medium sized bowl, mix mangoes with turmeric. Cover and set aside until mangos have absorbed the yellow turmeric colour. Heat corn oil on medium-high heat in a heavy-based pan until very hot. Add mustard seeds and fry until seeds jump and crackle in the pan. Gently shake the pan to prevent seeds from burning. Reduce heat to medium, add marinated mango and stir gently until mangos are soft. Remove mangos from heat and cool. Place ½ of the mango mixture, ½ tbsp nigella seeds and 2 chilli peppers into the sterilized jar. Repeat this process with the remaining mango mixture, nigella, salt and lime juice. Pour enough vinegar in jar to cover the mixture. Top with the rest of the chilli peppers. Seal jar and set outside under the sun for 10 days. Store in refrigerator but return to room temperature before eating.

EXECUTIVE CHEF DANNY KATTAR
ABU DHABI

'WHEN I WATCH MY GUESTS ENJOYING MY SWEET CREATIONS, I EXPERIENCE A GREAT MOMENT OF JOY.'

For this chapter I purposely decided to interview a chef of different origin, a Canadian Lebanese standout whom I chose as an exception to the rule for this book. He is not Emirati.

I chose Executive Chef Danny Kattar for the exceptional dessert creations he specially creates for the Emirati community. For this reason, he cannot be overlooked!

Executive Chef Kattar, a front line chef with an infectious smile is an artist and creator at the InterContinental Hotel in Abu Dhabi! This exceptional chef, a key player in the culinary world, is a master at combining traditional textures, flavours and tastes which result in elegant modern masterpieces!

From a Press Release: 'Chef Danny has over sixteen years of experience in the hospitality industry, having worked in numerous hotels in various countries around the world before his arrival to the United Arab Emirates. He joined InterContinental Hotels Group (IHG) in 2000 as part of the pre-opening team at InterContinental Phoenicia Beirut. He then moved to Malta and later to Doha where he held the position of Executive Sous Chef.

His first position as Executive Chef was in Kuwait and later at InterContinental Mzaar in Lebanon. Chef Danny was named one of six international jurors in Horeca Salon Culinaire in 2008. The following year he joined the pre-opening team at Crowne Plaza and Staybridge Suites, Yas Island in Abu Dhabi prior to his final destination at InterContinental Abu Dhabi. In 2013 he earned the title 'Executive Chef of the Year' at the Abu Dhabi Gourmet Stars Awards Gala dinner.'

A common friend of ours, Jasmine Haas from Germany, to whom I am forever grateful and who, at the time of this interview, was still working for the InterContinental Hotel in Abu Dhabi, introduced me to renowned Executive Chef Danny Kattar. What a privilege to be able to taste many of this highly acclaimed Chef's new pastry creations directly from his kitchen. The pastry creations originate from Lebanese cuisine with a subtle and elegant fusion between traditional Emirati and Lebanese flavours and an avant-garde style and look that he was working on for the new Lebanese restaurant 'Byblos-Sur-Mer'. It is located on the premises of the InterContinental Hotel in an astonishing waterfront setting.

His inspirations and intuitions turn into immediate hits amongst his large number of Emirati guests who enjoy eating with their families and guests. Executive Chef Kattar honoured me with a cooking demonstration for both of the selected desserts for my cookbook: *ithmaliyeh* and *aish al saraya*. According to Chef Kattar, these were designed with elegance in mind. They are light and fluffy, lightly sugared and infused with cardamom, pistachios, orange blossoms and rose-water. The nest-like design intensifies the look while the partially crisp on the outside, heavenly smooth on the inside completes this creation. The dessert was then topped with cream or custard, pine nuts, cashews, drizzled with date syrup and delicately sprinkled with orange blossoms.'

Celebrated Chef Danny continued: 'Emirati women enjoy sharing my large-portioned creations with their female friends and they keep coming for more. That is why I will give you the recipes for both Emirati-Lebanese desserts. When I observe my guests enjoying my creations I experience a great moment of joy as well,' said the accomplished chef.

I could not contain my enthusiasm and did not stop at 'tasting only'. I had one mouth-watering bite after another, a total of six large portions from the above-mentioned deserts. Admittedly, I was unable to eat dinner during our diplomatic function that evening, but it was worth it!

Bravo, Chef Kattar!

Aish Al Saraya

CUSTARD PASTRY DRIZZLED WITH ORANGE BLOSSOM SYRUP AND TOPPED WITH NUTS

SERVES 6–8

INGREDIENTS FOR SUGAR SYRUP:

1 cup sugar
1 tbsp candied orange blossoms
1 tbsp rose water
1 tbsp lemon juice
1 cup water
7 tbsp date paste or date syrup
7–8 slices toasted white bread, crust removed

INGREDIENTS FOR CUSTARD:

4 cups milk
200 ml condensed milk
1¼ cup whipping cream
2 tbsp rose water
2 tbsp candied orange blossoms
⅓ cup corn flour

INGREDIENTS FOR TOPPING:

¼ cup pistachios, slivered
¼ cup cashew nuts
¼ cup pine nuts
4 cups fresh cream, whipped
1–2 tsp date syrup for each dome
1–2 candied orange blossoms for each dome

Rose water and orange blossoms are commonly used in Middle Eastern culinary cuisine, and are availability in Western supermarkets and grocery stores in the 'ethnic foods' sections. They are also often available at health and natural food stores and grocers.

SUGAR SYRUP:

Place toasted bread evenly in a 9x9-inch (22x22-cm) square dish. In a large saucepan over low-medium heat, add sugar, water, and lemon and gently stir until the sugar dissolves completely. This may take 3–5 minutes. Add candied orange blossoms and rose-water and mix well. Pour hot syrup over toast in pan and allow to soak. Set aside until it has reached room temperature. Spread date paste or date syrup on top of soaked toast slices and set aside.

CUSTARD:

In a large saucepan on medium heat stir together milk, cream, condensed milk and corn flour. Stir until custard has reached a medium thick consistency. Once custard has thickened, add rose-water and candied orange blossoms. Stir more until custard has reached a thick pouring consistency. Portion the soaked bread on plates. Fill a piping bag with whipped cream. Make a whipped cream dome on each soaked bread portion. Pour custard over whipped cream dome.

TOPPING:

Decorate with pistachio, cashew and pine nuts. Top with date syrup and candied orange blossoms. Enjoy it alone or even better, share this exquisite pastry with your family and friends!

Ithmaliyeh Noodles

PASTRY NESTS FILLED WITH CUSTARD, ORANGE BLOSSOM SYRUP AND HONEY

SERVES 3–4

INGREDIENTS FOR ITHMALIYEH NOODLES:

280 g fresh *ithmaliyeh* noodles (or vermicelli noodles)
¼ cup butter

INGREDIENTS FOR SUGAR SYRUP:

1 cup sugar
1 tbsp candied orange blossoms
1 tbsp rose water
1 tbsp lemon juice
1 cup water

INGREDIENTS FOR CUSTARD:

4 cups milk
200 ml condensed milk
1 ¼ cup whipping cream
2 tbsp rose water
2 tbsp candied orange blossoms
⅓ cup corn flour
¾ cup nuts of your choice, ground

INGREDIENTS FOR TOPPING AND GARNISH:

1 tbsp candied orange blossoms
2.5 tbsp clear honey
¼ cup pistachios, slivered
½ cup cashew nuts
½ cup pine nuts

ITHMALIYEH NOODLES:

Cover cookie sheet with baking or parchment paper. Shape the noodles into approximately 3 cm high nests. Melt and pour butter onto each ithmaliyeh nest and bake at 180°C in the oven for 8 minutes or until golden. Remove nests from oven and soak each nest with sugar syrup and set aside.

SUGAR SYRUP:

In large saucepan over low-medium heat, add sugar, water, and lemon and stir until sugar mixture dissolves completely. This may take 3–5 minutes. Add candied orange blossoms and rose-water and mix well. Pour hot syrup over each ithmaliyeh nest and allow to soak. Set aside until it has reached room temperature.

CUSTARD:

In a large saucepan, stir together milk, cream, condensed milk and corn flour. Keep stirring until custard has reached a medium-thick consistency. Add rose-water and candied orange blossoms. Stir until the custard has reached a 'thick' pouring consistency. Remove from heat and set aside.

BASE:

Spread serving plates with the ground nut mixture. Carefully place nests on the layer of ground nuts. Spoon 1 portion of custard in each nest.

TOPPING AND DECORATION:

Garnish each nest with crushed pistachios, cashew and pine nuts. Top with honey and candied orange blossoms. A good Turkish coffee with a small glass of water or a strong espresso is recommended to complement this delightful dish.

AISHA AL MEHREZI
ABU DHABI

'IN MY HOME, COOKING OLD TRADITIONAL EMIRATI DISHES AND MODERN LIFE COEXIST IN HARMONY.'

I chuckle when I am given names and street numbers in Abu Dhabi as more often than not I am unable to find the streets. For this interview, I decided to take a taxi hoping the taxi driver would find the street in the Masafi district. Unfortunately, the driver was unable to follow my instructions. 'Madame, speak Nepalese, first client, first day me taxi driver in Abu Dhabi. Help me.'

Despite the 45°C temperature I left the taxi and walked to the Mehrezi villa. I asked a security guard to guide me to Aisha's villa. His reply was: 'Madame, too hot to walk, take taxi.' It took me ten minutes to reach the villa and by then, needless to say, my clothes were soaked!

Upon seeing me in drenched clothes a household assistant kindly showed me in the first living room where I paused to rest until I was ready to be welcomed by Aisha Al Mehrezi.

Ten minutes passed and I was glad to have been given time to cool down. A beautiful young woman stepped into the living room and asked me to follow her to the main *majlis* where a large table was laden with dates, seeds, fruits, tea, coffee and water. Once again, I was welcomed in the elegant Emirati food ritual to guarantee I felt comfortable in my new surroundings.

Aisha, a charming and self-assured young mother, introduced herself in a soft spoken voice and helped me acclimatize to the cooler temperature with hot tea and sugar.

I began the interview by asking Aisha about her family and children. She jumped right in and told me that her parents had the same last name 'Al Mehrezi' and they originated from the same tribe. Both parents were born and raised in Ras Al Khaimah, located in the northernmost coastal region of the United Arab Emirates. It is an emirate of camels, date farms and desert dunes. 'Trips to Ras Al Khaimah are a bi-monthly ritual for family and relatives.'

She continued: 'In Ras Al Khaimah, our traditional Emirati cuisine is known for its delicious homemade dishes which are still handed down from one generation to another. Today, our local Emirati values and food culture have evolved and in my home, cooking old traditional Emirati dishes, international dishes and modern life coexist in harmony.'

'I cook traditional Emirati dishes for my children with the help of our kitchen assistants. This leaves little time to do the vast amount of preparatory work for our traditional recipes. I am very lucky though as my sister-in-law roasts coffee beans for me and my mother prepares traditional Emirati butter known as *dehn kheneen* or ghee,' explained Aisha, 'and she also prepares numerous other traditional Emirati dishes that are labour intensive.'

'You may consider me a modern mother. But I place great importance on cooking authentic Emirati meals for my family. I am lucky to have a family who assists me in the preparation of traditional dishes to ensure that my children learn to respect our food culture.

I have five children of which two attend the German International School in Abu Dhabi (GISAD). We have decided that we will educate our children according to our own Emirati values as well as the German values that two of my children bring home from school!'

Aisha chose one of her favourite traditional Emirati drinks for this cookbook: the traditional Ras Al Khaimah coffee, also known as Emirati coffee, roasted by her sister-in-law, served with *chbaab*, an Emirati pancake like bread. I was invited to stay and taste both bread and the Ras Al Khaimah coffee which indeed were delicious! I had three chbaab. One with date syrup, one with honey and the last with white cheese which was washed down with numerous demi-cups of local coffee and tea.

Emirati Coffee

SERVES 6–8

⅓ cup ground coffee
4 cups water
1 tsp cardamom powder
1 pinch saffron threads

For roasting and grinding coffee beans see page 154.

For brewing the Emirati coffee on stovetop pour water in a medium pot and bring to a boil. Add freshly ground coffee and bring it to a boil. Simmer coffee for 15 minutes. While coffee is simmering, add cardamom and saffron to a thermos. Remove coffee from heat and pour into thermos. Infuse in thermos for 10 minutes before serving. Pour the Emirati Coffee with your left hand and hold the demi-cup in your right while filling it half full. Being served a half filled demi-cup offered with the right hand is a sign of respect. Remember: Emirati Coffee is usually served with dates!

NASRA ALBALOOSHI
ABU DHABI

FUSING TRADITIONAL AND MODERN EMIRATI LIFE

Meet Nasra, a young woman who enjoys training falcons with her family, cooking traditional Emirati dishes, experimenting with modern North American cake recipes while studying and working full time!

23-year-old Nasra Albalooshi graduated from the Sheikh Zayed University in 2015 with a major in International Affairs. She is a tall, warm hearted, intelligent and independent young woman who lives with her parents and seven siblings at their family home in Al Rahba, Abu Dhabi. We became good friends in the course of our interview.

Nasra proudly shared her family background. The young scholar is from Abu Dhabi, the nation's capital, while her father and his parents were from Al Ain, 150 kilometres to the southeast of the capital city.

Through Nasra, I was introduced to the culture and rituals of a newborn Emirati child. Nasra's cousin had just given birth to her first child. As a mother, she is celebrated and acknowledged for her delivery of a child. Shortly after Nasra's cousin gave birth I was invited to come celebrate their post-birth ritual at the hospital.

Nasra urged me to come as soon as possible in order to experience this magical ritual. Indeed it was! Nasra welcomed me with a big smile in the lobby of the Corniche Abu Dhabi Maternity Hospital. She then escorted me to the VIP Maternity Suite which was beautifully decorated with balloons and flowers. Ceiling high trays were heaped with individually wrapped chocolates in all flavour, size and shape, while other trays were laden with exotic and local fruits. Also present was an entourage of Philippinas who were diligently and personally looking after each guest who had come to wish Nasra's cousin the best for her first born child.

The Mother, who had given birth the evening before, welcomed me warmly. She had been attending to her guests since shortly after the birth. I was speechless and it felt wonderful being welcomed by Nasra's family. In fact, all guests were women as men are not permitted to attend this special 'post-birth ritual' unless the father of the child, brothers or uncles also attend. If men do enter, all the women simultaneously put on their head scarves or cover their faces. A moment of total unison amongst the women in the room!

I was invited to sit close to the mother who was disciplined not to show any sign of fatigue. She explained to me that she had personally chosen the decorations for the receiving room and her newborn child's crib and clothes.

Nasra made sure I would not go home hungry. She kept discreetly replenishing my tray with Lebanese 'Mezes', otherwise known as appetizers: a delightful assortment of sandwiches, fruits and julienned vegetables which she followed with a tray with dates.

What I enjoy the most is the exquisite Emirati coffee served in a demi-cup. The ritual is that upon having finished drinking, the holder of the cup jiggles it from right to left, indicating that she or he has had enough coffee. I decided not to jiggle too early. I was in such heaven appreciating the fragrances of cardamom, saffron and ginger in the coffee!

Many months later, we finally managed to meet and I was able to interview the youngest and charming traditional Emirati cook for my cookbook. Nasra decided to cook two of her favourite Emirati sweet dishes for my book: *habba hamra* (custard) and *sago* (a tapioca dish) usually served during Ramadan.

A delightful soothing and sweet cress seed drink. The seeds are also known as garden cress seeds.

Haba Hamra

GARDEN CRESS BEVERAGE

SERVES 6–8

¾ cup cress seeds
4 cups cold milk
½ cup sugar
¼ cup instant custard powder

In a medium sized pot mix cold milk, cress seeds, sugar and instant custard powder. Whisk well. Make sure there are no lumps in the mixture. Cook over medium heat. Continue stirring gently and bring mixture to a boil. Keep stirring to prevent mixture from sticking to the pot. Cook until mixture has thickened and has developed a gel-like consistency. Remove pot from heat. Spoon cooked haba hamra into tea cups. Serve warm or at room temperature.

Haba hamra custard drink is sweet, tastes like custard and the seeds are slightly crunchy, recommended to be served hot, while slowly sipping away the delicious creamy drink. *Haba hamra* can be spooned, due to its custard like consistency when cooled down. However *haba hamra* is not recommended for pregnant women.

This comfort sweet liquid custard drink is traditionally served to postpartum women and is also one of the most important drinks to the Emiratis while celebrating birth, weddings, Eid and for all other special occasions.

Sago Pudding

SERVES 6–8

1½ cups medium-sized sago pearls
4 cups water
½ cup sugar
1 pinch saffron threads
½ tsp cardamom powder
¼ cup sliced almonds, toasted

Sago is a starch extracted from the spongy centre or pith of the sago palm.

Soak sago in water for 15 minutes. Drain and rinse sago. In order to caramelize the sugar, place sugar in a deep saucepan on medium heat. Stir sugar with a wooden spoon and move the liquefied sugar from the edges to the centre of the pan until it has melted to avoid burning the sugar. Stir until sugar has turned amber or light brown in colour. This may take up to 10 minutes. Boil water on medium heat in a medium sized pot. For this step only, remove saucepan from heat and place on a wooden board. Carefully add hot water to caramelized sugar. It will sputter and bubble up vigorously.

Bring deep saucepan back to the heat. Add saffron and cardamom, stir and bring to a boil. Add drained sago to the boiling water. Simmer on medium-low heat. Keep stirring to prevent sago from sticking to the pot. Continue to cook until sago is fully translucent and the mixture has thickened. Spoon cooked sago into small custard cups. Sprinkle each cup with toasted, sliced almonds. Serve while still hot.

ZAHRA AL NAHDI
AL BATEEN, ABU DHABI

'THE ARABIC WORD '*QAHWA*' GAVE BIRTH TO THE WORD "COFFEE".'

Zahra Al Nahdi, a beautiful Emirati and a dear friend of mine, lived close to my villa in Al Bateen, Abu Dhabi. She welcomed us soon after our arrival in 2009 with a magnificent Emirati meal. My family and I devoured the rice biryani, then enjoyed her delicately prepared Emirati coffee flavoured with ample saffron and ginger. I realized that I was very privileged to meet Zahra. I was gifted with traditional Emirati dishes prepared and created by her! As the cook that I am, I couldn't be happier!

As we gradually got to know each other, I realized that the coffee ritual was an important part of Emirati life. Zahra told me that she always made sure to hand-pick her own green unroasted coffee beans from suppliers who kept fresh coffee beans aside especially for her. Zahra maintains it is essential to prepare freshly roasted coffee when serving guests. This is a sign of respect and deep subliminal acknowledgment when guests come to visit.

She also stresses the importance of the words 'respect', 'grounding' and 'acknowledgment' which are deeply rooted in the Islamic religion. She maintains that these words should be in the coming generation's vocabulary as essential tools in order for them to feel at peace amongst guests. As Zahra would say, when you apply these three essential values in your dealings with others, they become part of your life values.

'We all yearn for respect and acknowledgment. It is easy to gift them, supported as we are by the Emirati ritual of serving coffee to the guests,' Zahra tells me with an assured smile. The hostess or host, while serving the coffee, has learned to become very conscious of their guests' needs, feelings, and whether they have 'arrived' or 'grounded' themselves while sipping the coffee.

At this point in our conversation Zahra was ready to demonstrate how to roast green coffee beans.

Drinking Emirati coffee is different from other Arabic coffee, in fact it is made from green raw coffee beans, roasted very lightly and often prepared at home which became a strong symbol of hospitality.

Zahra stressed the importance of respecting Emirati coffee pouring etiquette which requires holding the *dallah* or coffee pot in our left hand and serving the demi-cups half full without a handle with the right hand.

Emirati coffee pouring etiquette is indeed a high form of communication amongst the Emiratis, signalling happiness, joy, relaxation, getting to know one another. It is also considered polite to be served an odd number of demi-cups with Emirati coffee, such as one, three etc.

'When we no longer desire to have our demi-cup refilled,' continued Zahra, 'we signal this to the host by jiggling the demi-cup from side to side when holding it between the fingers.'

Emirati coffee rituals take place in the *majlis*, meaning 'place of sitting', during their traditional feasts, special occasions such as weddings, Ramadan and Eid. These gatherings give the opportunity for Emiratis to communicate and connect with their families, the elderly and sheikhs. And not to forget: their business meetings always include Emirati coffee!

Qahwa

SERVES 6–8

3 tbsp ground coffee
3 cups water
2-cm-piece fresh ginger, peeled and ground to a paste

ROASTING ON STOVETOP AND GRINDING EMIRATI QAHWA:

Use a heavy frying pan dedicated for coffee roasting only as coffee has the capacity to absorb all odours. Pour 2 cups of Hariri Ethiopian green coffee beans in preheated frying pan. Stir slowly with a wooden spoon on medium heat to prevent burning, uneven roasting and sticking to the pan. After 10–15 minutes, coffee beans should start to turn a light brown in colour. They will start to crackle. Keep stirring! The outer shells or chaff will start to shed. Keep stirring until desired medium brown colour. Remove coffee beans from skillet and cool by tossing them in a large colander or pot. Once beans are cooled, put in an electric coffee mill used for coffee only. Grind 2 cups of freshly roasted coffee beans, 4 tbsp cardamom pods, and 1 teaspoon of saffron threads into a fine-texture similar to a Turkish coffee grind.

BREWING:

Pour water into a medium pot. Bring to a boil. Add freshly ground coffee and simmer for 20 minutes. Remove the pot from the stove and allow the coffee grounds to settle to the bottom of the pot. Pour the *qahwa* into a *dallah** or coffee pot and add the freshly pounded ginger. Serve.

SERVING:

Dallah is the Arabic name for the coffee pot specifically designed to pour the *qahwa*. Serving the *qahwa* from a *dallah*: With your left hand, pour *qahwa* in a demi-cup which you hold in your right hand. Only fill it half-full. It is considered respectful to be served a demi-cup half filled. This way one can drink the *qahwa* in three sips.

Zahra was so proud of her *qahwa* recipe that she proceeded to open a silver box full of delicious dates harvested from her friend's garden!

Legeimat

ONE-BITER MINI FLAT DOUGHNUTS

SERVES 6–8

This recipe has been personalized with the addition of mozzarella cheese by Zahra Al Nahdi. It is a fact that Emirati women often have long discussion as to whether this culinary gem is called *fgaa*, *khanfaroush* or *legeimat*! I was lucky enough to witness one of these legendary discussions between Zahra and her friend Umm Mohammed who is also featured in this cookbook. It seems that the aim of the discussion is not to reach a conclusion but to leave it vague enough so that it can continue at a next meeting. For the sake of continuity, I decided to use the word *legeimat* in this recipe. Whether *fgaa* or *legeimat*, this pastry is a delicious and traditional sweet similar to doughnuts and is often served during Ramadan and special occasions.

1 cup white flour
½ cup powdered milk
1 cup mozzarella cheese, grated
1 tbsp instant yeast
½ cup sugar
1 tsp saffron threads, soaked in ¼ cup hot water
2 tbsp oil
1–1¼ cup water depending on the type of flour used
¼ cup sesame seeds
½ cup date syrup
4 cups oil for frying

Mix dry ingredients and cheese in a large bowl. Add saffron and as much water needed to obtain a dough the consistency of soft cookie dough. Knead for at least 10 minutes. Let dough rest for 30 minutes. Roll out dough on a floured surface to 1 inch (2 cm) thickness. Using a 2.5-inch round cookie cutter cut as many rounds as possible. Heat oil in a deep pan over medium heat and drop 3–5 legeimat into the hot oil. Using a large metal spoon, turn the legeimat over to get an even golden colour. Place them on a platter. Drizzle with date syrup and sprinkle with sesame seeds. Best eaten while warm. Watch out! Zahra's fluffy, sweet legeimat may persuade you to eat without sharing!

AYSHA KHAMIES AL KHADDEIM
DIBBA, AL FUJAIRAH

'I AM A SCHOOL TEACHER WHO ENJOYS PARTICIPATING IN COOKING COMPETITIONS.'

Finding Aysha Khamies Al Khaddeim's villa in Dibba, Al Fujairah turned out to be another challenge! Thank Allah, my good friend Azza Al Qubaisi was there to help me. Both of us laughed because we realized that we had been challenged numerous times before.

After a thirty-minute search we decided to call Aysha for directions. We had to look for alternative routes as certain streets and roads remained closed or were rerouted to make way for new villas being constructed.

In her sweet calm voice, she simply instructed us to follow the construction site and to look out for her head, covered in a long black and gold scarf which would be sticking out above the large metal portal.

And indeed there was Aysha, waiting for us like in a Shakespearean theatre, her covered head slightly tilted, a welcoming smile on her face and the rest of her body hidden behind the portal! For a moment, I felt I was the audience and Aysha was up on stage!

This was to be the second last interview for this book. The long-established welcoming tradition of Emirati hospitality still impressed me! Aysha and her sisters reflected beauty, honesty, kindness and open heartedness as they welcomed us as 'VIP's! We were greeted and led into one of Aysha's sister's large ladies' reception areas known as *majlis* and welcomed with hot and cold drinks, fruits and dates.

Aysha is a natural performer with seventeen years' experience as a school teacher at the Al-Taweyeen and Safiya Bint Huyai School in Dibba. Aysha smiled and proudly started the interview: 'I enjoy cooking and preparing new Emirati recipes for every competition. My family, relatives and friends get to taste my recipes before I submit the final work to the judges.'

Aysha proudly showed us the 18 Carat Gold food award she won in the 'Emirati Amateur Chefs' category during the 2014 Dubai World Hospitality Championships. She was amongst the first winners. The International Competition's organization falls under the directives of His Highness Sheikh Hamdan bin Mohammed bin Rashid Al Maktoum, Crown Prince of Dubai. In fact, that's where I first met Aysha.

Smiling, she went on to explain that her parents are both from the Al Dhanhani tribe originally from Dibba, Al Fujairah, which is the largest town in the Northern part of the Emirate. 'I have seven sisters and six brothers,' she added warmly.

Aysha continued: 'Cooking requires a lot of patience and time just like teaching and learning. In fact, I think that cooking, teaching and learning are virtually the same experience. I enjoy preparing lessons, teaching students, and finally getting rewarded when I correct their tests. The same is true when I spend hours following recipes resulting in dishes that will be savoured by everyone!'

'I design, prepare and cook traditional Emirati dishes which require experience based on the ingredients used. My mother taught me to use the freshest ingredients, and to balance the spices needed for each dish. In our food tradition we use a lot of saffron which compels us to judge the exact amount necessary to respect our Emirati food rituals. Emiratis enjoy eating in respect to the food rituals such as the tactile (touch), gustatory (taste), olfactory (smell) and visual experience.'

Aysha prepared two sweet dishes for my book: *Rangila*, meaning colourful in Hindi, and *khabees*, a semolina dish. Aysha's words of recommendation: 'You will love these dishes. This is your chance to ignore the calories and let yourself indulge in all these favourite Emirati sweet treats, perfect for breakfast, snacks or dessert.'

During the evening we were served dinner, as is customary in the Emirates, on a colourful tablecloth placed on the floor with over twenty different dishes that the mother and sisters had prepared prior to our arrival. Once again, needless to say I felt an overwhelming sense of gratitude for the immense amount of work, care and attention on the part of the ladies for our welcome. A pure culinary delight!

Khabees

SERVES 5–10

Khabees is a delectable sweet traditional dessert enjoyed for breakfast, snack, and especially during Eid. It is often served as part of the *fualah* rituals when guests or families gather in the afternoon or mid-morning.

2½ cups semolina
2½ cups water
1 cup white sugar
1 tsp butter
2 tbsp oil
¼ tsp saffron powder
¼ tsp saffron threads
1 tbsp cardamom powder
½ tsp ginger powder

Put the semolina in a heavy skillet and place over medium heat. Stir the semolina constantly while it is toasting so it will not burn! For a medium toast similar to light caramel colour, it will take 5–7 minutes, then set aside and cover. In a separate pot add water, sugar, butter, oil, saffron powder and threads, cardamom, ginger and stir until butter has melted. Simmer while stirring for another 5 minutes. Add the toasted semolina. Continue to stir constantly for an additional 5 minutes or until *khabees* is dry. Fill each dessert dish with *khabees*, leaving room at the top. *Khabees* may be stored in an airtight container in the refrigerator for up to 3 days.

Don't forget to make yourself an Emirati coffee while slowly enjoying the delicious *khabees* until there is none left to share!

Rangila

TOASTED FLOUR LAYERED WITH PUREED DATES

SERVES 10–20

In this recipe the dates become the base and flour mixture the topping, in contrast to the traditional recipe *batheetha* which incorporates pureed dates in the flour mixture.

1 kg frozen Halali dates (or fresh dates of your choice), pitted
200 g butter
1 cup all-purpose flour
1 tbsp cardamom powder

Thaw frozen dates (if using frozen). Process in batches in blender until very smooth. Place 4 tbsp (use 2 tbsp if using small dish) pureed date in each dessert dish, cover and set aside. Put flour in a heavy skillet and place over medium heat. With a whisk stir the flour constantly while it is toasting so it will not burn! For a medium toast similar to light caramel colour, it will take 5–7 minutes. Add butter and stir until butter has melted. Add powdered cardamom. Mix well. Remove from heat. Cover each date-filled dish with toasted flour mixture, leaving room at the top. Place rangila in the refrigerator until ready to eat.

Rangila, a variation of batheetha is a delicious dessert. You won't believe how wonderful it tastes until you have tried it! Both children and adults enjoy this traditional Emirati dish. To add to the goodness, remember that this dish is prepared without sugar!

LATIFA TAYEEB AL KHAJA
SHARJAH

'HENNA GET-TOGETHERS AND ENJOYING TRADITIONAL EMIRATI SWEET DISHES IS A WOMAN'S TIME TO EMPOWER HERSELF AND OTHERS.'

Early during the interview, Latifa stated that the focus of our interview would be to describe her family's Henna get-togethers and the art of henna applications. Since the interview was about food, she also agreed to share her family's favourite traditional Emirati sweet dish.

Latifa, a dignified and elegant woman with strong noble features, was looking forward to passing on her story for my book. She thought it very relevant because it reflects the majority of Emirati women who enjoy getting together for henna designing day. Most often the gatherings take place at home. However, they are increasingly taking place in luxury hotels in preparation for festive events such as weddings, births or for regular henna maintenance.

'These get-togethers allow women to be in a special space where they can chat about upcoming weddings, partner matches, children and family issues and updates, but especially remain informed. It's an Emirati tradition passed on from the time we were living as Bedouins in the desert.'

'Henna get-togethers are a woman's time to re-connect by creating a deeper bond with herself and empower others. We take time for ourselves to feel emotionally nourished by other women, while henna designers, known as *al mehanaya*, apply natural henna dye in simple traditional geometric patterns on the palm of the hand or intricate floral and geometric Indian designs on the back of the hand. The *al mehanaya* women were originally hired so as to avoid staining one's own finger when applying the henna. Today however, most designers apply henna directly from a hand-held flexible plastic tube.'

Henna or *Lawsonia Inermis* is a flowering non-edible shrub used to make dye. They are often seen growing in the gardens of Emirati families who harvest the leaves while green and leave them to gradually dry in the sun. When thoroughly dry, the leaves are pounded and sifted to a fine powder then mixed with the liquid of cooked dry limes. In the past, drops of petrol were incorporated. Latifa told me that she still blends her henna mixture with cooking liquid from dry limes but admits having dropped the petrol. She also covers the paste with a little water to protect it from drying, then leaves it to rest until the desired colour appears.

These henna preparations were to ensure a deep black hue which is still the preferred colour. Modern women acquire henna mainly from India, Somalia and Oman. Often the designers are Ethiopian, Baluchistani, Moroccan, Somali, Minau, Pakistani and Indian. Commercially bought black henna contains toxic chemicals and is no longer being sold. However, natural plant-based and organic henna is readily available.

Latifa reflected: 'Emirati women still associate henna with long life, protection from the heat and sun, good luck, health, beauty, sensuality, and amongst some of the older women, the ability to heal. Modern Emirati women consider henna designs to be a sign of beauty and sensuality but especially a personal statement.'

Latifa continued to say: 'I prefer to use the traditional method of applying henna. I often use one of my favourite designs known as *rawayid*. You recognize a *rawayid* design when you see that the woman's fingers have been either dipped or covered in henna as far as the first finger joint including the nails. In the centre of the palm, a large circle representing the moon and the sun or a half moon with a dot on the right is drawn. Women often connect the design with a line to the thumb and some connect henna to all the fingers.

Connecting the design on the palm originated from the design called *gassah* which came from the time when women held the henna paste in a closed palm until it was completely dry. This method inevitably caused all fingers including the nails and half of the hand to be covered with henna, thus all fingers inside the palm are connected to the thumb and vice versa. The *gassah* design is rarely used today but can be seen amongst older women.

My mother and my grandmother used to have to lie on the sofa for many hours until the henna dried on their hands and feet. Henna on the feet was very soothing, especially during the hot season when we had no air conditioners. Women either hennaed their entire feet up to the ankles, and hands up to the wrist in a ghamsah design or had only their soles and toes covered in henna; this was known as rawayid design.'

While Latifa was applying henna on her hands and describing its design history, we both enjoyed her family's favourite sweet dishes. The desserts had been prepared by her kitchen staff prior to my arrival. Latifa proudly told me that she personally taught her staff most of her family's recipes which had been passed on by her ancestors.

Then with a nostalgic reflection, Latifa went on to describe her family's background: 'Long before the discovery of oil, my family lived in Sharjah and Dubai where my grandfather was in the pearl industry. He owned his pearling boat with eight to ten divers or ghasah, eight to ten haulers known as siyub and additional assistants. My grandfather also mentioned that he had a singer on board known as a naham. The naham sang rhythmical chants of encouragement in order to alleviate the hard tasks and work on board the vessel during pearling season.'

The pearling industry was my grandfather's passion and a full time occupation. Between seasons he would travel to India and other countries to sell his treasures. Unfortunately for my grandfather, the pearling industry came to an end in the 1930's due to the economic depression of that time. We were very fortunate that my grandfather's income from the pearling industry could support our family into the next generation. From that point on, pearling was replaced by a good education.'

Latifa finished her henna work on her hands and with a broad smile moved over to sit next to me. She shared her henna recipe but most importantly her family Emirati dessert recipe. What a delightful experience for me!

Khabees

SEMOLINA CRUMBLE DESSERT WITH SAFFRON, CARDAMOM AND ROSE WATER

SERVES 10

450 g semolina
9 tbsp ghee
1 cup sugar
2 cups water
255 g very thin, short noodles
1 tbsp cardamom powder
½ tsp saffron threads
5½ tbsp rose water
¼ cup nuts of your choice, chopped and toasted
¼ cup raisins

Preheat oven to 100°C. Add semolina to a heavy pot over medium-low heat and dry roast it. Stir frequently to prevent burning. Continue stirring until light brown in colour and semolina gives off a light toasted fragrance. Add 6 tbsp ghee and stir until butter has melted. Mix water and sugar, pour into semolina and stir frequently until liquid is absorbed. Add remaining ghee and continue stirring. Add thin short noodles and mix well. Add powdered cardamom, saffron and rose-water. Mix well. Remove skillet from heat and transfer semolina to an ovenproof baking dish. Cover and bake for 30 minutes. Check for doneness. Semolina should taste soft and fluffy. If not, bake a little longer and check again. When done, remove from oven and add nuts and raisins. Mix well. Place *khabees* in dessert dishes and serve warm or cold.

ACKNOWLEDGEMENTS

To my brother Baron Anatol von Hahn, without whose financial support I would not have been able to realize my dream of writing *Culinary Magic of the Emirates*.

To those involved in the 'technical' part of my cookbook: Motivate Publishing, my publisher, as well as everyone who helped produce the earlier blueprint of the book: Don MacIver, Johanna Warham, Dorthe Naumann, Silke Berreth and Diane Laflamme-Millette, who helped to design, shape and produce *Culinary Magic of the Emirates* into a beautiful cookbook.

To Azza Al Qubaisi for sharing her contacts and for driving me across the United Arab Emirates with her family.

To Dr Frauke Heard-Bey, author of *From Trucial States to United Arab Emirates*, for assisting me with her knowledge and expertise on the Emirates.

Words cannot express my gratitude to my beloved family and close friends, Baron Peter von Hahn-Lieven and Countess Marie Jeanne Sennyey-Széchenyi, Mathias von Polenz, Tamara von Polenz, Nikolai von Polenz, Jason MacCallum, Marina-Désirée von Anrep, Amal Obaid Al Mazrouie, Jasmine Haas, Karin von Rosenbach, Loluck Baby, Dr Petra Scheunemann, Bettina Lebrun, Zahra Al Nahdi and Yvonne Arnold. Also to everyone else whom I have not mentioned, for this book would not have been possible without their support and encouragement.

KITCHEN EQUIVALENTS

METRIC TO US CONVERSION

1 ml	=	1/5 teaspoon
5 ml	=	1 teaspoon
30 ml	=	1 fluid oz.
100 ml	=	3.4 fluid oz.
240 ml	=	1 cup
1 litre	=	34 fluid oz.
1 litre	=	4.2 cups
1 litre	=	2.1 pints
1 litre	=	1.06 quarts
1 litre	=	.26 gallon
1 gram	=	.035 ounce
100 grams	=	3.5 ounces
500 grams	=	1.10 pounds
1 kilogram	=	2.205 pounds
1 kilogram	=	35 oz.